TEST YOUR TERROR

TRIVIA FROM THE DARK SIDE OF HISTORY

JOE MYNHARDT

Published by Crystal Lake Publishing
Where Stories Come Alive!

Crystal Lake Publishing
www.CrystalLakePub.com

Join the Crystal Lake community today on our newsletter and Patreon!
https://linktr.ee/CrystalLakePublishing

Download our latest catalog here.
https://geni.us/CLPCatalog

ISBN: 978-1-968532-22-2

Cover art:
Joanna Halerz—jo.widomska@gmail.com

Layout:
Lori Michelle Booth—www.theauthorsalley.com

Follow us on Amazon:

WELCOME
TO ANOTHER

CRYSTAL LAKE PUBLISHING
CREATION

INTRODUCTION
WELCOME TO THE DARK SIDE OF TRIVIA

Do you dare dive into the abyss of forgotten facts, eerie events, and twisted truths?

Test Your Terror is your gateway to the macabre side of history, fiction, and true crime. With 459 hand-picked questions, this book isn't just a trivia game—it's a tour through humanity's haunted halls, shadowy basements, and cursed past.

Inside these pages, you'll encounter:
- True stories more disturbing than fiction
- Creepy rituals, murder mysteries, and haunted movie sets
- Trivia about your favorite horror books, movies, and real-life monsters

Some questions are deadly serious. Others are darkly funny. Some will test your knowledge of ancient myths, while others ask if you remember which actor lost a limb in some movie.

Perfect for solo brain-teasing on the toilet or a scream-worthy game night with your friends.

So light the candles. Lock the doors. And prepare to *test your terror. . .*

HOW TO PLAY ON GAME NIGHT

Grab your most fearless friends and follow these steps for a horrifyingly fun trivia night:

Choose a Host: One person reads the questions and keeps score. Preferably someone with a sinister laugh.

Decide on a Format:
- Individual: Each person answers questions on their own.
- Teams: Split into groups—like Vampires vs. Werewolves. Fight to the (quiz) death.

Points System:
- Correct Answer = 1 Point
- For Multiple Choice and True/False, only one guess allowed.

Winner Gets Bragging Rights—or a cursed artifact. Your call. You can even appoint rewards according to each person's ranking.

RANKING SYSTEM
ARE YOU A HORROR HISTORIAN. . . OR FRESH MEAT?

After answering all 459 questions, total your score and see where you fall on the scale of sinister smarts:

SCORE	TITLE	DESCRIPTION
0-50	**Fresh Meat**	You've barely stepped into the shadows. Maybe keep the lights on. . .
51-150	**Curious Corpse**	You're digging up bones and facts, but the crypt is still deeper.
151-200	**Occult Observer**	You've seen things. Maybe too much. You're whispering with witches now.
201-300	**Grave Scholar**	You're quoting *The Necronomicon* and arguing horror lore for fun.
301-400	**Terror Archivist**	A walking encyclopedia of fear. Are you even still human?
401-459	**The Eldrich One**	You've *mastered* all. The abyss is impressed. You've become the horror.

LET THE GAMES BEGIN

QUIZ

1. In which 1980 slasher film did Kevin Bacon play a memorable role as one of the killer's victims?

    A. Prom Night
    B. Friday the 13th
    C. My Bloody Valentine
    D. The Burning

2. What was the nickname given to the mechanical shark used in *Jaws*?

    A. Big Mike
    B. Jaws Jr.
    C. The Great White Machine
    D. Bruce

3. In which year did the mysterious disappearance of the Roanoke Colony occur?

    A. 1492
    B. 1587
    C. 1620
    D. 1701

4.True or False: The Winchester Mystery House has over 160 rooms, built to confuse ghosts.

5. The _____ Plague of 1518 involved people dancing uncontrollably until they collapsed or died.

ANSWERS

1. B. Friday the 13th

Kevin Bacon appeared in *Friday the 13th* (1980) as Jack, one of the ill-fated counselors at Camp Crystal Lake. His character's gruesome death scene, involving an arrow through the throat while lying on a bunk, is one of the film's most iconic moments. Though he became a Hollywood star with films like *Footloose*, his horror roots remain a favorite topic among genre fans.

2. D. Bruce

The mechanical shark used in *Jaws* was nicknamed "Bruce" after Steven Spielberg's lawyer, Bruce Ramer. The shark famously malfunctioned throughout filming, which inadvertently made the movie scarier by forcing Spielberg to use the shark sparingly and rely on suspenseful shots and John Williams' iconic score.

3. B. 1587

In 1587, a group of English settlers established the Roanoke Colony on Roanoke Island, in what is now North Carolina. Led by John White, the colony was intended to be the first permanent English settlement in the New World. When White returned from England in 1590 after a delayed resupply trip, he found the colony deserted with no clear signs of what had happened to its inhabitants. The word "CROATOAN" was carved into a post, suggesting they may have moved to a nearby island, but no definitive evidence was ever found. This unsolved mystery has inspired countless theories, from assimilation with Native tribes to supernatural explanations like curses or alien abductions.

4. True

The Winchester Mystery House, located in San Jose, California, is a sprawling mansion with over 160 rooms, staircases that lead to nowhere, doors that open into walls, and windows overlooking other rooms. Built by Sarah Winchester, heiress to the Winchester rifle fortune, the house was under constant construction for 38 years. Sarah believed she was haunted by the spirits of those killed by Winchester rifles and thought that continuously expanding the house would confuse the ghosts and protect her. The mansion's bizarre design has made it a popular tourist attraction and a fascinating piece of paranormal history.

5. Dancing

The Dancing Plague of 1518 was a bizarre and unexplained phenomenon that occurred in Strasbourg, in modern-day France. It began when a woman started dancing in the street and couldn't stop. Within days, dozens of others joined her, seemingly unable to control their movements. Some danced for weeks, collapsing from exhaustion, and even dying from strokes or heart attacks. Local authorities, believing it to be caused by demonic possession or divine punishment, hired musicians to encourage the dancing in hopes of relieving the curse. Modern theories suggest it may have been caused by ergot poisoning, stress-induced mass hysteria, or other psychological factors, but the true cause remains a mystery.

QUIZ

6. Match these historical figures to their spooky reputation:

   A. Vlad the Impaler   1. Blood Countess
   B. Elizabeth Báthory   2. Dracula inspiration
   C. Grigori Rasputin   3. Voodoo Queen
   D. Marie Laveau   4. Mystic Monk

7. In what year were the Shirley Jackson Awards established, and what event inspired their creation?

   A. 2000, to commemorate the centennial of Shirley Jackson's birth
   B. 2007, to honor her legacy in psychological suspense and dark fiction
   C. 2010, following the release of a documentary about her life
   D. 1995, during the inaugural World Horror Convention

8. What hidden chamber was discovered beneath the Great Pyramid of Giza in 2017 using advanced scanning technology?

   A. The King's Secret Room
   B. The Grand Gallery Void
   C. The Pharaoh's Treasure Room
   D. The Hall of Records

ANSWERS

6.
A. 2 ~ *Dracula inspiration*
B. 1 ~ *Blood Countess*
C. 4 ~ *Mystic Monk*
D. 3 ~ *Voodoo Queen*

- **Vlad the Impaler (Dracula inspiration):** Vlad III of Wallachia, known for impaling his enemies on stakes, earned his fearsome nickname and inspired Bram Stoker's iconic vampire, Dracula. While some see him as a tyrant, others regard him as a national hero for defending his people.
- **Elizabeth Báthory (Blood Countess):** This 16th-century Hungarian noblewoman was accused of torturing and killing young girls. Legends claim she bathed in their blood to maintain her youth, though much of her story may have been exaggerated by political enemies.
- **Grigori Rasputin (Mystic Monk):** A Russian mystic and advisor to Tsarina Alexandra, Rasputin was rumored to have supernatural powers. His controversial influence over the royal family and his mysterious, prolonged death added to his sinister legend.
- **Marie Laveau (Voodoo Queen):** A famous practitioner of Voodoo in 19th-century New Orleans, Marie Laveau was revered and feared for her spiritual practices and influence. Her legacy lives on in folklore, with many still believing in her mystical powers.

7. *B. 2007, to honor her legacy in psychological suspense and dark fiction*

The Shirley Jackson Awards were established in 2007 to recognize outstanding achievements in psychological suspense, horror, and dark fiction. The awards pay tribute to Shirley Jackson, whose work, including *The Lottery* and *The Haunting of Hill House*, remains a cornerstone of the genre. The awards were created to fill a gap in recognizing the more psychological and literary aspects of dark storytelling.

8. *B. The Grand Gallery Void*

In 2017, researchers discovered a previously unknown void above the Grand Gallery of the Great Pyramid of Giza using muon tomography, a scanning technique. While its purpose remains unclear, the void adds to the enduring mysteries surrounding the construction and function of the pyramid.

QUIZ

9. Which hotel in California is infamous for its alleged hauntings and dark history, including the death of Elisa Lam?

   A. The Cecil Hotel
   B. The Overlook Hotel
   C. The Roosevelt Hotel
   D. The Chateau Marmont

10. True or False: The Paris Catacombs hold the remains of over six million people.

11. _____ Castle in Scotland is rumored to have a secret room where the bones of a family were discovered.

12. What Facebook livestream in 2016 claimed to capture a ghostly figure walking through a historic mansion?

   A. The Winchester Walkthrough
   B. The Haunted Mansion Ghost
   C. The Myrtles Plantation Specter
   D. The Riddle House Haunting

ANSWERS

9. A. *The Cecil Hotel*

The Cecil Hotel, located in downtown Los Angeles, has a grim reputation as one of the most haunted and infamous hotels in the world. Opened in 1924, it has been the site of numerous murders, suicides, and mysterious deaths. Its notoriety grew further in 2013 with the chilling case of Elisa Lam, whose body was found in a rooftop water tank after she was seen acting strangely in elevator security footage. The Cecil Hotel also housed serial killers like Richard Ramirez, the "Night Stalker," and Jack Unterweger, adding to its eerie allure. This combination of dark history and paranormal activity has made it a frequent subject of documentaries, books, and ghost investigations.

10. *True*

Beneath the streets of Paris lies a vast network of tunnels known as the Catacombs, which house the bones of over six million people. In the late 18th century, Paris's overflowing cemeteries posed a public health risk, prompting authorities to transfer remains to the abandoned limestone quarries beneath the city. Arranged in haunting displays of skulls and bones, the Catacombs stretch for miles, creating an underground ossuary that attracts millions of visitors annually. The dark and labyrinthine passages have inspired countless ghost stories and urban legends, solidifying their place in history as one of the most macabre attractions in the world.

11. *Glamis*

Glamis Castle, located in Angus, Scotland, is one of the most famous haunted locations in the British Isles. The castle is steeped in legend, including tales of a hidden room where the bones of a murdered family were allegedly found. It's also associated with Macbeth, as it served as the fictional setting for Shakespeare's tragedy. Visitors and staff have reported ghostly apparitions, strange sounds, and eerie sensations throughout the castle. Among its most chilling legends is the story of the "Monster of Glamis," said to be a deformed heir kept hidden in the secret chambers. These tales make Glamis Castle a hauntingly popular site for paranormal enthusiasts.

12. C. *The Myrtles Plantation Specter*

A visitor livestreamed their tour of The Myrtles Plantation in Louisiana, known for its haunted reputation. During the stream, viewers spotted a ghostly figure in a mirror and shadowy movements in the background. The livestream quickly went viral, with paranormal enthusiasts dissecting the footage.

QUIZ

13. Which horror film reportedly had a cursed set, where a light fixture fell on the actor playing a demonic entity and a glass light exploded during filming—leading to the entire set being blessed by a priest?

    A. The Nun
    B. The Exorcism of Emily Rose
    C. Annabelle
    D. Hereditary

14. True or False: A YouTube video titled *My Apartment is Haunted* gained millions of views after capturing a shadow figure moving across the screen.

15. True or False: The Tunguska Event of 1908 was caused by an alien spacecraft crash.

16. The unexplained "Wow! Signal" was detected by astronomers in which year?

ANSWERS

13. C. Annabelle

While filming Annabelle (2014), a series of unsettling accidents put everyone on edge. A heavy light fixture crashed down on the actor portraying the demonic force, and during another scene, a glass light shattered unexpectedly near the same spot. Tension grew so thick they called in a priest to bless the set—because when your horror movie starts acting like a horror movie, it's time for holy water.

14. True

The video, uploaded by a user claiming to experience paranormal activity, showed unexplained movements, shadowy figures, and strange noises. The authenticity of the footage sparked heated debates in the comments, dividing viewers between believers and skeptics.

15. False. Most scientists believe it was a meteor explosion.

The Tunguska Event occurred on June 30, 1908, when a massive explosion flattened over 800 square miles of forest in Siberia, Russia. Witnesses reported seeing a bright fireball streaking across the sky, followed by a deafening blast. The explosion is widely believed to have been caused by a meteor or comet fragment exploding mid-air at an altitude of 3–6 miles. Despite the absence of an impact crater, the energy released was estimated to be 1,000 times more powerful than the atomic bomb dropped on Hiroshima. While some conspiracy theories suggest alien involvement, no evidence supports this claim, and the Tunguska Event remains a fascinating example of the Earth's vulnerability to cosmic phenomena.

16. 1977

The "Wow! Signal" was a strong, narrowband radio signal detected by astronomer Jerry R. Ehman on August 15, 1977, while working on a SETI (Search for Extraterrestrial Intelligence) project at Ohio State University. The signal, originating from the Sagittarius constellation, lasted 72 seconds and was so unusual that Ehman wrote "Wow!" in the margin of the data printout. Despite extensive searches, the signal has never been detected again, leaving scientists and enthusiasts to wonder if it was a message from an alien civilization or a natural cosmic anomaly. The mystery of the "Wow! Signal" remains unsolved, sparking debates and inspiring countless works of science fiction.

QUIZ

17. What is the name of the group of children who band together to fight Pennywise in Stephen King's *It*?

    A. The Derry Seven
    B. The Losers' Club
    C. The Misfit Gang
    D. The Defenders of Derry

18. What gruesome invention was used to execute William Wallace, the inspiration for *Braveheart*?

    A. The Rack
    B. Drawing and Quartering
    C. The Judas Chair
    D. The Pear of Anguish

19. True or False: The guillotine was still in use in France until the 1970s.

20. The man responsible for designing the first atomic bomb was _____.

ANSWERS

17. B. The Losers' Club

The Losers' Club is the heart of Stephen King's *It*, consisting of seven children who confront their deepest fears to battle the sinister Pennywise. Their bond and bravery are central to the story, making them some of King's most beloved characters.

18. B. Drawing and Quartering

William Wallace, the Scottish freedom fighter who inspired the film *Braveheart*, met a brutal end in 1305 after being captured by the English. He was subjected to drawing and quartering, one of the most horrific execution methods of the medieval era. This punishment involved being hanged, disemboweled while still alive, and then dismembered into four parts, which were displayed across the kingdom as a warning. Wallace's defiance and tragic death made him a symbol of Scottish resistance, immortalizing him as a national hero and a martyr for freedom.

19. True

The guillotine, synonymous with the French Revolution, was used as an official execution method in France until 1977. Its last use was to execute Hamida Djandoubi, a convicted murderer, on September 10, 1977, in Marseille. The guillotine was praised in its early years as a humane and egalitarian form of capital punishment but became a grim symbol of the Reign of Terror. Capital punishment was abolished in France in 1981, marking the end of the guillotine's infamous history. Its longevity is a chilling reminder of the device's lasting legacy.

20. J. Robert Oppenheimer

J. Robert Oppenheimer, often called the "Father of the Atomic Bomb," led the scientific team of the Manhattan Project during World War II. Under his direction, the first nuclear bomb was developed and successfully tested on July 16, 1945, in New Mexico—a test codenamed "Trinity." After witnessing the devastating power of the bomb, Oppenheimer famously quoted the Hindu scripture, *Bhagavad Gita*: "Now I am become Death, the destroyer of worlds." Though his work helped end the war, it also ushered in the nuclear age, a legacy that haunted Oppenheimer for the rest of his life.

QUIZ

21. What Egyptian artifact is believed to bring a curse upon anyone who disturbs it?

    A. The Rosetta Stone
    B. King Tutankhamun's Tomb
    C. The Great Sphinx
    D. The Dendera Light

22. In which country did the infamous "Red Rain" fall in 2001, baffling scientists?

    A. India
    B. Brazil
    C. China
    D. Australia

23. True or False: The Bell Witch haunting inspired the movie *The Blair Witch Project*.

24. The strange "Mothman" sightings in the 1960s were reported in _____, West Virginia.

ANSWERS

21. B. King Tutankhamun's Tomb

The discovery of King Tutankhamun's tomb in 1922 by Howard Carter sparked rumors of a curse after several individuals involved in the expedition died under mysterious circumstances. While most deaths can be explained by natural causes, the so-called "Curse of the Pharaohs" remains a compelling legend tied to ancient Egypt's treasures.

22. A. India

The "Red Rain" phenomenon occurred in Kerala, India, between July and September 2001. The rain's unusual red color was caused by microscopic particles, initially thought to be dust or algae spores. Some theories even suggested extraterrestrial origins, claiming the particles might be alien microbes brought by a meteor. While further analysis indicated they were terrestrial in origin, likely spores of local algae, the event sparked widespread fascination and debate, making it a favorite topic for both scientific inquiry and conspiracy theories. The "Red Rain" remains an intriguing natural mystery.

23. True

The Bell Witch haunting is one of America's most famous ghost stories, originating in Adams, Tennessee, in the early 19th century. The Bell family claimed they were tormented by a violent and intelligent spirit that could speak, move objects, and even physically attack them. The haunting culminated in the death of John Bell, which the spirit allegedly took credit for. This legend inspired various films and media, including *The Blair Witch Project*. Though *The Blair Witch Project* presents a fictional narrative, its concept of an unseen, malevolent force in the woods draws clear parallels to the Bell Witch legend, blending folklore with modern horror storytelling.

24. Point Pleasant

The Mothman, a mysterious creature with glowing red eyes and large wings, was first reported in Point Pleasant, West Virginia, in 1966. Numerous sightings occurred over the following year, with witnesses describing a humanoid figure that could fly at incredible speeds. The Mothman became linked to the tragic collapse of the Silver Bridge in December 1967, which killed 46 people. Many believe the creature was an omen of disaster, while skeptics attribute the sightings to misidentified birds or mass hysteria. The legend of the Mothman endures, inspiring books, movies, and an annual festival in Point Pleasant.

QUIZ

25. Which ruler was known as "The Impaler?"

    A. Ivan the Terrible
    B. Vlad III of Wallachia
    C. Attila the Hun
    D. Genghis Khan

26. A viral TikTok video by @iamcaden captured a mysterious creature in a forest, sparking comparisons to the _____.

27. The 2010 film *The Rite*, starring Anthony Hopkins, was inspired by the true story of Father Gary Thomas, a Catholic priest trained in _____.

28. True or False: Some skeletons found at Machu Picchu had elongated skulls, possibly due to intentional cranial deformation.

29. What 1972 movie was inspired by the survival story of a rugby team stranded in the Andes after a plane crash?

    A. Alive
    B. Deliverance
    C. The Grey
    D. Cast Away

ANSWERS

25. B. Vlad III of Wallachi

Vlad III, also called Vlad the Impaler, ruled Wallachia in the 15th century and gained infamy for his brutal tactics, particularly impaling his enemies on wooden stakes. This gruesome method of punishment earned him his chilling nickname and a fearsome reputation. Vlad's reign was marked by his fierce defense against the Ottoman Empire, making him a national hero in Romania despite his cruelty. His legend became the inspiration for Bram Stoker's *Dracula*, cementing his place in history as one of the most notorious figures of the medieval period. Vlad's dark legacy continues to fascinate and terrify people worldwide.

26. Wendigo

@iamcaden's TikTok showed a shadowy, humanoid figure in a remote forest. Many viewers speculated it was a Wendigo, a creature from Native American folklore. The eerie video fueled theories about cryptids and unexplained phenomena, although skeptics argued it was likely staged.

27. Exorcism

The Rite is based on the real-life experiences of Father Gary Thomas, whose training as an exorcist included confronting claims of demonic possession. The film explores the psychological and spiritual challenges of exorcism, blending fact with dramatization to create a chilling narrative.

28. True

Cranial deformation was a common practice among the Inca elite to signify social status. Elongated skulls found at Machu Picchu suggest that high-ranking individuals lived or were buried there, adding an eerie layer of mystery to the site's purpose and the rituals performed there.

29. A. Alive

Alive is based on the true story of Uruguayan Air Force Flight 571, which crashed in the Andes in 1972. Stranded for 72 days, the survivors resorted to cannibalism to stay alive. The film captures the harrowing ordeal and the resilience of the human spirit under extreme conditions.

QUIZ

30. True or False: The movie *Primal Fear* was inspired by a real case of a defendant pleading insanity to avoid conviction.

31. The 1975 thriller *Dog Day Afternoon* was inspired by a real bank robbery committed by _____.

32. What inspired the idea for the killer doll in *Child's Play*?

    A. A haunted doll legend
    B. A popular "My Buddy" doll
    C. A ventriloquist dummy
    D. A malfunctioning toy robot

33. True or False: The original *Halloween* was filmed on a shoestring budget of just $300,000.

34. What was the original working title for *Friday the 13th*?

    A. Camp Blood
    B. The Long Night at Crystal Lake
    C. A Long Night of Fear
    D. A Mother's Revenge

35. True or False: Michael Myers was originally called "The Shape" in the *Halloween* script.

ANSWERS

30. True

Primal Fear (1996), starring Edward Norton and Richard Gere, drew inspiration from real-life cases where defendants claimed insanity as a defense. While the film itself is fictional, its plot reflects the moral and legal complexities of such cases, leaving audiences questioning justice and truth.

31. John Wojtowicz

Dog Day Afternoon is based on John Wojtowicz's 1972 attempted bank robbery in Brooklyn, New York. Wojtowicz's motive was to fund gender reassignment surgery for his partner. The botched robbery turned into a hostage situation and media spectacle, immortalized by Al Pacino's riveting performance in the film.

32. B. A popular "My Buddy" doll

The *Child's Play* series was inspired by the popular "My Buddy" dolls of the 1980s, which some children found creepy. Writer Don Mancini combined this idea with the concept of voodoo and possession to create Chucky, one of horror's most iconic villains.

33. True

John Carpenter's *Halloween* was made on a tight budget of $300,000. To save money, the crew used cheap props, including the infamous Michael Myers mask, which was a modified William Shatner mask purchased for less than $2. The low budget didn't stop the film from becoming a genre-defining classic.

34. A. Camp Blood

The working title *Camp Blood* referred to the gruesome murders at Camp Crystal Lake. The film's final title, *Friday the 13th*, was chosen for its ominous and superstitious connotations, cementing its place in horror history.

35. True

In the script and credits for *Halloween*, Michael Myers was referred to as "The Shape" to emphasize his inhuman and abstract presence. This title reflected his role as a faceless embodiment of evil rather than a typical character.

QUIZ

36. In *Child's Play*, the serial killer who possesses Chucky's body is named Charles Lee Ray, a combination of the names of infamous criminals Charles Manson, Lee Harvey Oswald, and _____.

37. What inspired Jason Voorhees' iconic hockey mask in *Friday the 13th Part III*?

   A. A mask found in a storage room
   B. The director's childhood sports gear
   C. A costume designer's idea
   D. A crew member's Detroit Red Wings fan gear

38. What 2020 TikTok series featured a user documenting their encounters with a mysterious "neighbor" who left cryptic messages and bizarre gifts?

   A. The Keyhole Diaries
   B. The Bunker Man
   C. The Neighbor's Notes
   D. The Other Side of the Wall

39. True or False: Wes Craven based Freddy Krueger's look on a homeless man he saw as a child.

40. What 2011 film about a haunted dybbuk box is based on a real-life paranormal claim?

   A. The Possession
   B. Annabelle
   C The Conjuring
   D. The Babadook

41. True or False: The movie *We Need to Talk About Kevin* was inspired by a real school shooting.

ANSWERS

36. James Earl Ray

The name Charles Lee Ray was a nod to three infamous figures: Charles Manson, Lee Harvey Oswald (JFK's assassin), and James Earl Ray (MLK's assassin). This chilling homage added a sinister edge to Chucky's already malevolent persona.

37. A. A mask found in a storage room

The iconic hockey mask was discovered by chance in a storage room on set. The design team modified it to create Jason's signature look, which has since become one of the most recognizable symbols in horror.

38. D. The Other Side of the Wall

A TikTok user shared videos of strange occurrences involving notes and small objects left outside their apartment. Viewers speculated about the identity of the "neighbor," with theories ranging from a stalker to an elaborate hoax. The suspense kept viewers hooked as the story unfolded.

39. True

Wes Craven designed Freddy Krueger's appearance based on a childhood memory of a homeless man who frightened him by staring through his bedroom window. This unsettling encounter stayed with Craven, inspiring Freddy's burned, grotesque face and eerie demeanor.

40. A. The Possession

The Possession tells the story of a cursed dybbuk box, said to contain a malicious spirit from Jewish folklore. The real-life dybbuk box, purchased on eBay, gained notoriety after its owner reported strange and terrifying phenomena. The film explores the concept of possession with a cultural twist.

41. False

While *We Need to Talk About Kevin* (2011) captures the emotional aftermath of a fictional school shooting, it is not directly based on real events. However, its exploration of maternal guilt, societal blame, and the psychology of violence resonates with real-life tragedies, making it a deeply unsettling and poignant film.

QUIZ

42. What acclaimed novel by modern horror author Alma Katsu reimagines the tragic Donner Party expedition with a supernatural twist?

    A. The Hunger
    B. The Deep
    C. The Fervor
    D. The Winter People

43. Adolf Hitler survived over _____ assassination attempts during his reign.

44. Which 1987 horror movie featured the Cenobites and the infamous line, "We have such sights to show you"?

    A. Hellraiser
    B. Phantasm II
    C. The Lost Boys
    D. Prince of Darkness

45. What is said to haunt the Tower of London?

    A. Anne Boleyn
    B. Guy Fawkes
    C. Queen Victoria
    D. Jack the Ripper

ANSWERS

42. A. The Hunger

Alma Katsu's *The Hunger* is a chilling blend of historical fiction and supernatural horror, reimagining the doomed Donner Party as they encounter something far more sinister than harsh winter conditions. Katsu's work stands out for its atmospheric storytelling and innovative twists on historical events.

43. 40

Adolf Hitler, the leader of Nazi Germany, survived more than 40 assassination attempts during his time in power. These attempts ranged from minor sabotage efforts to meticulously planned plots, including the infamous July 20, 1944, Valkyrie plot led by German military officers. In that incident, a bomb placed in a conference room detonated but failed to kill Hitler due to the placement of the briefcase carrying the explosives. His survival fueled his belief in destiny and invincibility, further bolstering his grip on power. These failed attempts highlight the intense opposition to his regime, even from within Germany.

44. A. Hellraiser

Clive Barker's *Hellraiser* introduced audiences to the Cenobites, otherworldly beings who explore pain and pleasure. The film's grotesque imagery and Pinhead's iconic presence left an indelible mark on 80s horror.

45. A. Anne Boleyn

Anne Boleyn, the second wife of King Henry VIII, was executed at the Tower of London in 1536. Her ghost is said to roam the grounds, sometimes carrying her severed head under her arm. The Tower, steeped in centuries of bloody history, is one of the most haunted locations in England, with numerous reports of eerie encounters and ghostly figures.

QUIZ

46. True or False: The Stanley Hotel, the inspiration for Stephen King's *The Shining*, is located in Colorado.

47. The famous Amityville Horror house is located in _____, New York.

48. Match these haunted locations to their spooky reputation:

A. Eastern State Penitentiary	1. Most haunted house in England
B. The Queen Mary	2. Prison ghost sightings
C. Borley Rectory	3. Haunted ship
D. The Myrtles Plantation	4. Plantation with 12+ spirits

ANSWERS

46. True

The Stanley Hotel, located in Estes Park, Colorado, inspired Stephen King to write *The Shining* after he and his wife stayed there in 1974. King experienced unsettling dreams and was struck by the hotel's eerie atmosphere, which later became the foundation for the Overlook Hotel in his iconic novel. The Stanley is also rumored to be haunted, with reports of ghostly children playing in the halls and the spirit of the original owner, F.O. Stanley, lingering in the building.

47. Amityville

The *Amityville Horror* house, located at 112 Ocean Avenue in Amityville, New York, gained infamy after the Lutz family claimed to experience terrifying paranormal activity there in 1975. This occurred just a year after Ronald DeFeo Jr. murdered six members of his family in the same house. Their story inspired books, movies, and endless debates about whether the haunting was real or a hoax. Despite its dark history, the house remains a fascination for fans of paranormal lore.

48.
A—Prison ghost sightings
B—Haunted ship
C—Most haunted house in England
D—Plantation with 12+ spirits

- **Eastern State Penitentiary:** This former Philadelphia prison is notorious for ghostly sightings, including shadowy figures and eerie whispers in its abandoned cells. Its grim history and harsh punishments make it a hotspot for paranormal investigators.
- **The Queen Mary:** This luxury liner turned floating hotel in California is famous for ghostly apparitions, including a "lady in white" and sightings in the ship's pool area. It's often called one of the most haunted ships in the world.
- **Borley Rectory:** Dubbed "the most haunted house in England," this rectory in Essex was plagued by poltergeist activity, spectral nuns, and mysterious writing on the walls before it was destroyed by fire in 1939.
- **The Myrtles Plantation:** Located in Louisiana, this plantation is rumored to be haunted by at least 12 spirits, including Chloe, a former enslaved woman, and the ghostly children she cared for. Its haunted reputation draws visitors from around the world.

QUIZ

49. What was the name of the infamous case involving mysterious green children who appeared in a 12th-century English village?

    A. The Enfield Poltergeist
    B. The Green Children of Woolpit
    C. The Bell Witch Incident
    D. The Beast of Gévaudan

50. True or False: Amelia Earhart's disappearance was definitively linked to a crash near Howland Island.

51. The Dyatlov Pass incident occurred in 1959 in the _____ mountains.

52. What is the name of the Japanese ghost story about a vengeful spirit haunting a well and appearing through a cursed videotape in modern adaptations?

    A. Okiku's Well
    B. Sadako's Curse
    C. The Ring
    D. Yotsuya Kaidan

53. Which of the following was NOT a real mystery?

    A. The Lost Colony of Roanoke
    B. The Bermuda Triangle
    C. The Vanishing of Flight 19
    D. The Phantom Train of Chicago

ANSWERS

49. B. The Green Children of Woolpit

The Green Children of Woolpit appeared in a small English village during the 12th century. According to legend, the two children had green skin, spoke an unknown language, and claimed to come from a place called "St. Martin's Land," where the sun never shone. Over time, their skin color faded, and the girl integrated into society, but the mystery of their origins remains unsolved. This strange tale continues to fascinate historians and folklorists alike.

50. False

Amelia Earhart's disappearance in 1937 during her attempt to circumnavigate the globe remains one of the greatest unsolved mysteries of the 20th century. While many theories suggest her plane crashed near Howland Island, no definitive evidence has ever been found. Speculation ranges from a simple crash at sea to more exotic theories involving espionage or survival on a remote island. The mystery of her fate continues to intrigue historians and adventurers.

51. Ural

The Dyatlov Pass incident took place in the Ural Mountains of Soviet Russia, where nine experienced hikers died under mysterious circumstances. Their tent was found ripped from the inside, and their bodies displayed bizarre injuries, including missing tongues and unexplained trauma. Despite numerous theories, from avalanches to UFOs, the true cause of their deaths remains a chilling mystery.

52. A. Okiku's Well

Okiku's Well is the origin of the classic Japanese ghost story *Banchō Sarayashiki*. Okiku was a maid unjustly killed by her master, and her spirit haunts the well where her body was thrown, counting dishes she failed to return. Modern adaptations like *The Ring* have reimagined this tale for contemporary audiences.

53. D. The Phantom Train of Chicago is fictional.

The Lost Colony of Roanoke: In 1590, the entire English settlement of Roanoke vanished, leaving behind only the cryptic word "Croatoan" carved into a tree.
The Bermuda Triangle: This infamous region in the Atlantic Ocean is linked to numerous unexplained disappearances of ships and planes.
The Vanishing of Flight 19: In 1945, a squadron of U.S. Navy bombers disappeared over the Bermuda Triangle, sparking theories of magnetic anomalies and alien abductions.
The Phantom Train of Chicago: While Chicago has its fair share of ghost stories, the Phantom Train is purely fictional, invented to keep you on your toes!

QUIZ

54. Who is credited with inventing the guillotine?

    A. Dr. Joseph-Ignace Guillotin
    B. Marquis de Sade
    C. Louis XVI
    D. Maximilien Robespierre

55. The original electric chair was designed by _____, a dentist.

56. What is the central theme of Adam Nevill's novel *The Ritual*, which was adapted into a 2017 horror film?

    A. A cursed artifact in a small town
    B. A group of friends encountering an ancient evil in the wilderness
    C. A haunted mansion with a sinister past
    D. A demon targeting a dysfunctional family

57. Match these eerie inventions to their purpose:

    A. Thumbscrew   1. Burn alive.
    B. Heretic's Fork   2. Silence "nags"
    C. Brazen Bull   3. Finger torture
    D. Scold's Bridle   4. Neck punishment

ANSWERS

54. A. Dr. Joseph-Ignace Guillotin

Dr. Joseph-Ignace Guillotin did not actually invent the guillotine but advocated for its use as a more humane method of execution during the French Revolution. The device was named after him due to his proposals for its implementation. Ironically, Guillotin opposed the death penalty in principle, but his association with the machine immortalized his name in one of history's darkest chapters.

55. Alfred Southwick

Alfred Southwick, a dentist by trade, designed the first electric chair in the 1880s as a supposedly more humane method of execution. His design was inspired by witnessing an accidental death caused by electric shock. The electric chair was first used in 1890, and while controversial, it became a staple of capital punishment in the United States for decades.

56. B. A group of friends encountering an ancient evil in the wilderness

Adam Nevill's *The Ritual* follows a group of friends on a hiking trip in the Scandinavian wilderness who stumble upon a strange cult and an ancient, godlike creature. The novel is celebrated for its chilling atmosphere, themes of guilt and survival, and its visceral horror, which translated effectively to the film adaptation.

57.
  A—Finger torture
  B—Neck punishment
  C—Burn alive
  D—Silence "nags"

- **Thumbscrew:** A medieval torture device that crushed the fingers, often used to extract confessions. Its simplicity made it a favorite tool of inquisitors.
- **Heretic's Fork:** A metal rod with sharp prongs at both ends, placed between the chin and chest or neck to prevent movement. It was used to punish heretics and ensure they couldn't sleep.
- **Brazen Bull:** An ancient execution device where victims were locked inside a hollow brass bull and burned alive. The design amplified their screams to sound like the bellowing of the bull.
- **Scold's Bridle:** A humiliating device used in medieval Europe to silence outspoken women, often referred to as "nags" or "scolds." It included a metal gag that prevented speech and symbolized the misogyny of the era.

QUIZ

58. What TikTok video showed an unsettling humanoid figure lurking on a remote beach, leading viewers to speculate about cryptids?

A. The Montauk Monster
B. The Beach Walker
C. The Siren Call
D. The Long Island Lurker

59. Which political figure reportedly saw Abraham Lincoln's ghost in the White House?

A. John F. Kennedy
B. Harry Truman
C. Theodore Roosevelt
D. Winston Churchill (while visiting)

60. The legend of the Flying _____ has long been associated with Cape Town's Table Bay, with sailors claiming to see it during storms.

61. True or False: The "Devil's Footprints" of 1855 were found in France.

62. In the legend of _____, villagers sacrificed a child to stop a plague in Hamelin, Germany.

ANSWERS

58. C. The Siren Call

A TikTok user captured footage of a shadowy humanoid figure near the ocean, with many claiming it resembled a siren or mermaid. The video's eerie soundtrack and shaky quality added to its mystique, sparking debates about cryptid sightings versus clever editing.

59. D. Winston Churchill

Winston Churchill, while staying as a guest in the White House during World War II, famously claimed to have encountered the ghost of Abraham Lincoln. According to the story, Churchill had just emerged from a bath, wearing nothing but a cigar, when he saw Lincoln standing by the fireplace in his room. Churchill, ever quick-witted, reportedly said, "Good evening, Mr. President. You seem to have me at a disadvantage," before the apparition vanished. Numerous other sightings of Lincoln's ghost have been reported in the White House, particularly in the Lincoln Bedroom, cementing his spectral presence as a fixture of presidential lore.

60. Dutchman

The legend of the Flying Dutchman involves a ghost ship doomed to sail the seas forever, often sighted off the coast of South Africa's Table Bay. The ship's captain, cursed for defying a storm, is said to bring misfortune to those who see it. The story has inspired countless adaptations in literature and film.

61. False. They were found in England.

The "Devil's Footprints" appeared after a heavy snowfall in Devon, England, on the night of February 8, 1855. These mysterious, hoof-like tracks stretched for over 100 miles, traversing rooftops, walls, and frozen rivers as if something otherworldly had walked straight through the countryside. Locals were terrified, believing the footprints to be evidence of the Devil himself. While some theorized they were caused by animals, a prank, or unusual weather, the event remains unexplained, capturing imaginations as one of England's eeriest mysteries.

62. The Pied Piper

The legend of the Pied Piper of Hamelin dates back to the Middle Ages and tells of a mysterious figure who rid the town of rats by playing his enchanted flute. When the townsfolk refused to pay him for his services, the Pied Piper lured the town's children away, never to be seen again. Some versions of the story suggest the Piper was avenging the town's mistreatment of outsiders, while others interpret it as an allegory for a plague or a historical migration event. Though largely a folk tale, the chilling imagery of children vanishing en masse has made the Pied Piper a haunting symbol of broken promises and retribution.

63. Only one of these is a real supernatural event. Can you spot it?

    A. The Salem Werewolf Trials
    B. The Warminster "Thing"
    C. The Loch Ness UFO Crash
    D. The Spectral Duel of Savannah

64. What is the name of Crystal Lake's official YouTube channel for kids?

    A. The Always Awesome Adventures of Eddie
    B. Doctor Frankensdice
    C. The Scareville Army
    D. The Eddie Poe Show

65. True or False: Linnea Quigley, known as a Scream Queen, starred in *Return of the Living Dead* and became synonymous with 80s horror.

66. What was the name of the ship found adrift in 1872 with its crew mysteriously missing?

    A. The Flying Dutchman
    B. The Mary Celeste
    C. The HMS Terror
    D. The Essex

63. B. The Warminster "Thing" was a real event.

The Warminster "Thing" refers to a series of mysterious sounds and sightings reported in Warminster, England, during the 1960s. Witnesses described strange noises like sonic booms, metallic screeches, and even unexplained flying lights in the sky. The phenomenon gained significant attention, attracting UFO enthusiasts and paranormal investigators. While some explanations suggest military testing or natural phenomena, no definitive cause has been identified. The Warminster "Thing" remains one of the most intriguing cases of unexplained events in modern history, with some dubbing the town "Britain's UFO capital" during its peak.

64. D. The Eddie Poe Show

Launched in 2025, The Eddie Poe Show is a fun and spooky adventure that brings books to life! A 10-year-old Edgar Allen Poe, Tina the worm, and Bones the cat travel into different stories, both new and classic, and embark on wild, whimsical, and occasionally eerie adventures.

65. True

Linnea Quigley's role as Trash in *Return of the Living Dead* (1985) is a standout performance in zombie horror. Quigley's energetic presence and appearances in films like *Night of the Demons* (1988) and *Silent Night, Deadly Night* (1984) made her a beloved figure in cult horror.

66. B. The Mary Celeste

The Mary Celeste was discovered drifting in the Atlantic Ocean, intact but without any sign of its crew. Despite extensive investigations, no definitive explanation has ever been found. Theories range from mutiny and piracy to strange weather phenomena or sea monsters. The ship's ghostly fate continues to captivate historians and mystery enthusiasts alike.

67. True or False: The Tunguska Event of 1908 was caused by an alien spacecraft crash.

68. What is one of the eeriest facts about horror writer Ambrose Bierce?

    A. He was struck by lightning while writing a ghost story
    B. He claimed to have been possessed while writing "An Occurrence at Owl Creek Bridge"
    C. He disappeared without a trace after joining a war
    D. He was buried alive during a séance stunt gone wrong

69. True or False: In 1915, Stonehenge was sold to a private buyer at auction.

70. True or False: No one was injured during the filming of *The Texas Chainsaw Massacre* (1974).

71. What infamous true crime case inspired Jack Ketchum's controversial novel *The Girl Next Door*?

    A. The Manson Family murders
    B. The Sylvia Likens case
    C. The Jonestown massacre
    D. The Zodiac killings

72. Sheridan Le Fanu was known for writing ghost stories steeped in Catholic guilt, Irish folklore, and chronic _____.

ANSWERS

67. *False*

The Tunguska Event was a massive explosion that flattened 800 square miles of Siberian forest. Most scientists believe it was caused by a meteor or comet fragment exploding in the atmosphere, but with no impact crater ever found, it remains shrouded in mystery. The incident is often referenced in conspiracy theories about alien encounters.

68. *C. He disappeared without a trace after joining the Mexican Revolution in 1913 as an observing journalist*

Ambrose Bierce, author of macabre tales like *An Occurrence at Owl Creek Bridge*, vanished in 1913 after crossing into Mexico to observe the revolution. No confirmed trace of him was ever found, fueling decades of speculation, conspiracy theories. . .and ghost stories.

69. *True*

In 1915, Stonehenge was sold to a private buyer, Cecil Chubb, for £6,600 at an auction. He later donated it to the British government in 1918. This transaction ensured the preservation of one of the world's most iconic prehistoric sites.

70. *False*

Filming conditions were brutal. The low budget meant actors had to wear the same sweat-drenched, gore-caked clothes every day in the sweltering Texas summer—sometimes in 100°F+ heat. Several scenes, including one involving a real finger being cut, were done for real after prop effects failed. The stench, injuries, and exhaustion added a level of realism (and misery) that's still talked about today. It was horror—in front of *and* behind the camera.

71. *B. The Sylvia Likens case*

Jack Ketchum's *The Girl Next Door* was based on the horrifying real-life case of Sylvia Likens, a teenager tortured and murdered in 1965 by her caregiver and others. The novel is notorious for its graphic depiction of cruelty, earning Ketchum a reputation as one of the most provocative authors in modern horror.

72. *Insomnia*

Le Fanu suffered from extreme insomnia, especially after the sudden death of his wife. His sleepless nights may have helped fuel the atmosphere of dread and melancholy in *Carmilla*, one of the first lesbian vampire tales in Western fiction.

QUIZ

73. True or False: Elizabeth Báthory, also known as the Blood Countess, was convicted of killing over 600 young girls.

74. Which 1981 film by Sam Raimi introduced audiences to the Necronomicon and the character Ash Williams?

    A. Dead by Dawn
    B. The Evil Dead
    C. Night of the Demons
    D. Phantasm II

75. What is said to haunt the Stanley Hotel, the inspiration for Stephen King's *The Shining*?

    A. A piano-playing ghost
    B. Disembodied children's laughter
    C. Shadowy figures in the halls
    D. All of the above

76. True or False: While filming *The Nun* (2018) in a Romanian fortress, the director reportedly saw a mysterious man walking the halls on security monitors—yet no one was actually there.

77. Which strange job did Algernon Blackwood ***not*** do before becoming a renowned writer of supernatural fiction?

    A. Reporter
    B. Hotel night clerk
    C. Farmer in Canada
    D. Secret agent for British Intelligence

ANSWERS

73. False

Elizabeth Báthory, a Hungarian noblewoman, was accused of torturing and killing dozens of young girls in the late 16th and early 17th centuries. Though convicted of 80 murders, folklore inflated this number to over 600. Legends claim she bathed in the blood of virgins to retain her youth, though historians debate the accuracy of these tales.

74. B. The Evil Dead

Sam Raimi's *The Evil Dead* became a cult classic for its over-the-top gore, innovative camera work, and Bruce Campbell's iconic portrayal of Ash Williams. The film's success spawned sequels, a TV series, and a devoted fanbase.

75. D. All of the above

Located in Estes Park, Colorado, the Stanley Hotel has a reputation for paranormal activity. Guests and staff have reported ghostly music from an empty ballroom, eerie laughter, and apparitions wandering the halls. Stephen King's stay at the hotel inspired him to write *The Shining*, cementing its place as a horror landmark.

76. True

Cameras don't lie. . . unless you're making a horror movie in an ancient Romanian fortress. While shooting *The Nun*, director Corin Hardy claimed he saw a man strolling through a monitor feed—but when he went to check, the corridor was empty. The crew got so spooked they started refusing to be alone in certain parts of the set. That's when you know you've nailed the atmosphere—maybe a little too well.

77. B. Hotel night clerk

Before Algernon Blackwood terrified readers with classics like *The Willows* and *The Wendigo*, he lived a life almost as strange as his stories. He worked as a reporter, ran a failed Canadian farm, and later *actually served in British intelligence*! He also dabbled in the occult, joining the Hermetic Order of the Golden Dawn. Not exactly your average horror author résumé.

QUIZ

78. True or False: Arthur Machen, author of *The Great God Pan*, was fired from his newspaper job because he kept turning every assignment into a horror story.

79. True or False: The original *Psycho* novel was written by Stephen King.

80. True or False: Area 51 is located in Roswell, New Mexico.

81. True or False: Borley Rectory, often called "the most haunted house in England," burned down in the 1940s.

82. What nickname was given to the unidentified serial killer active in London in 1888?

   A. The Night Stalker
   B. Spring-heeled Jack
   C. Jack the Ripper
   D. The Midnight Butcher

ANSWERS

78. False—but it *sounds* true.

While he didn't get fired for scaring readers, Arthur Machen *did* cause a media frenzy during WWI with his fictional story *The Bowmen*, which readers believed was a true account of angelic soldiers helping British forces. He accidentally created a national myth. Oops.

79. False

Although King is the undisputed king of horror, *Psycho* was written by Robert Bloch in 1959, which was later turned into a movie by Alfred Hitchcock.

80. False

This is a common mix-up. Roswell is where the infamous 1947 UFO crash reportedly happened. But Area 51—the ultra-secretive military base—is in Nevada. Still, both places are shrouded in aliens, secrecy, and enough tinfoil to keep a conspiracy theorist cozy.

81. True

Borley Rectory was infamous for reports of poltergeists, ghostly nuns, and phantom footsteps. Built in the 19th century, it became a hub for paranormal investigations in the early 20th century. After a mysterious fire in 1944, it was demolished, but its reputation endures as one of England's most chilling haunted locations.

82. C. Jack the Ripper

Jack the Ripper is the pseudonym for an unidentified murderer who terrorized London's Whitechapel district. Known for gruesomely killing and mutilating women, the killer was never caught. Over a century later, the case remains one of the most famous unsolved mysteries, with endless theories about the perpetrator's identity.

QUIZ

83. True or False: The disappearance of the Flannan Isles lighthouse keepers in 1900 is explained by a rogue wave washing them away.

84. Who is the author of the 2022 bestseller novel, *The Exorcist's House*?

   A. Stephen King
   B. Nick Roberts
   C. Graham Masterton
   D. Duncan Ralston

85. In 1692, the Salem Witch Trials were sparked by what alleged phenomenon?

   A, Possession by demons
   B. Ergot poisoning
   C. A curse from a slave
   D. Mysterious fits and convulsions

86. True or False: The Mothman, a winged creature with glowing red eyes, was seen before the collapse ofthe Silver Bridge in West Virginia.

87. What eerie feature makes the Winchester Mystery House famous?

   A. Doors leading to nowhere
   B. Staircases ending at ceilings
   C. An obsession with the number 13
   D. All of the above

ANSWERS

83. *False*

In December 1900, three lighthouse keepers vanished from the remote Flannan Isles off Scotland. Their disappearance left clues such as an uneaten meal and an overturned chair. While a rogue wave is a plausible theory, no definitive evidence exists, leaving the mystery unsolved and steeped in speculation.

84. *B. Nick Roberts*

Nick Roberts is the author of *The Exorcist's House*, a gripping modern horror novel that blends supernatural chills with haunting family secrets. The story revolves around a family who moves into an old farmhouse, only to discover its dark history tied to an exorcist's tragic past. The book has been praised for its atmospheric writing, spine-chilling moments, and homage to classic supernatural horror.

85. *D. Mysterious fits and convulsions*

The Salem Witch Trials began when young girls in Salem, Massachusetts, displayed strange symptoms such as fits, screaming, and contortions. Accusations of witchcraft followed, leading to the execution of 20 people. Modern theories suggest the girls' behavior may have been caused by psychological stress or ergot poisoning, a fungus found in rye bread.

86. *True*

Sightings of the Mothman in Point Pleasant, West Virginia, in 1966 and 1967 coincided with a series of strange events and ended with the collapse of the Silver Bridge, killing 46 people. Many believe the Mothman was an omen of disaster, while skeptics attribute the sightings to misidentified birds or hysteria.

87. *D. All of the above*

Built by Sarah Winchester, heiress to the Winchester rifle fortune, this sprawling mansion in San Jose, California, is a labyrinth of bizarre architecture. Sarah believed she was haunted by spirits of those killed by Winchester rifles and built the house to confuse them. Today, it's a popular destination for ghost hunters.

QUIZ

88. True or False: The Myrtles Plantation in Louisiana is said to be haunted by the ghost of a slave named Chloe.

89. Which historical figure mysteriously vanished during their reign?

   A. Napoleon Bonaparte
   B. King Edward V of England
   C. Cleopatra
   D. Julius Caesar

90. True or False: The Voynich Manuscript, an illustrated codex written in an unknown language, was decoded in 2020.

91. What was the purpose of the Brazen Bull, a torture device used in ancient Greece?

   A. Psychological torment
   B. Burning victims alive
   C. Public humiliation
   D. Crushing bones

92. True or False: The Iron Maiden was widely used during medieval times to torture prisoners.

93. Who was the infamous Soviet leader known for purges and mass executions during then Great Terror?

   A. Leon Trotsky
   B. Nikita Khrushchev
   C. Joseph Stalin
   D. Vladimir Lenin

94. True or False: Genghis Khan was responsible for the deaths of more people than any other historical figure.

ANSWERS

88. True

The Myrtles Plantation is often called one of America's most haunted homes. Legend has it that Chloe, a slave, poisoned the plantation owner's family, resulting in her own death by lynching. Her spirit is said to linger, appearing in photographs and causing eerie disturbances.

89. B. King Edward V of England

Edward V and his brother, Richard, were the Princes in the Tower, confined to the Tower of London in 1483. They disappeared, and their fate remains a mystery. Many suspect their uncle, Richard III, had them killed to secure his claim to the throne.

90. False

The Voynich Manuscript, created in the 15th century, remains one of the world's greatest literary mysteries. Its strange script and illustrations defy interpretation, and no one has definitively deciphered its meaning, leading to endless theories about its origin and purpose.

91. B. Burning victims alive

The Brazen Bull was designed by Perillos of Athens for the tyrant Phalaris. Victims were locked inside the hollow metal bull, and a fire was lit beneath it, roasting them alive. The design amplified their screams to sound like the roar of a bull. Ironically, Perillos himself was reportedly the device's first victim.

92. False

Contrary to popular belief, the Iron Maiden is likely a myth. While it's a staple in horror imagery, historical evidence suggests it was fabricated in the 18th century to create a lurid view of medieval punishment. No accounts of its actual use exist from medieval times.

93. C. Joseph Stalin

During the Great Terror of the 1930s, Stalin's regime executed or imprisoned millions accused of being enemies of the state. His use of fear and propaganda consolidated his power but left a legacy of unparalleled brutality in Soviet history.

94. True

Genghis Khan's conquests in the 13th century resulted in the deaths of an estimated 40 million people, reshaping Eurasia. Despite his fearsome reputation, he also facilitated cultural exchange and trade across his vast empire, known as the Pax Mongolica.

QUIZ

95. Which iconic horror writer is often referred to as the "Master of the Macabre"?

    A. Stephen King
    B. Edgar Allan Poe
    C. H.P. Lovecraft
    D. Shirley Jackson

96. True or False: Mary Shelley wrote *Frankenstein* as part of a ghost story competition.

97. The Cthulhu Mythos, a shared universe of cosmic horror, was created by _____.

98. What is the name of the haunted hotel in Stephen King's *The Shining*?

    A. The Overlook Hotel
    B. The Stanley Hotel
    C. The Bates Motel
    D. The Marsten House

99. True or False: Bram Stoker's *Dracula* was the first vampire novel ever written.

100. Who wrote the story "The Lottery," a chilling tale of small-town ritualistic violence.

ANSWERS

95. B. Edgar Allan Poe

Edgar Allan Poe is celebrated as one of the pioneers of modern horror and Gothic literature. His works, such as *The Tell-Tale Heart, The Fall of the House of Usher*, and *The Raven*, explore themes of madness, death, and the supernatural. His legacy has influenced countless authors and remains an integral part of the horror genre.

96. True

In 1816, during a stay at Lake Geneva with Lord Byron and Percy Shelley, Mary Shelley conceived the idea for *Frankenstein*. The group had challenged each other to write ghost stories, and Mary's vision of Dr. Frankenstein creating life became the basis for her groundbreaking novel, which is considered the first science fiction story.

97. H.P. Lovecraft

H.P. Lovecraft introduced the Cthulhu Mythos in his stories, creating a universe filled with ancient, incomprehensible entities. Works like *The Call of Cthulhu* and *At the Mountains of Madness* explore themes of humanity's insignificance in a vast, indifferent cosmos. Lovecraft's mythos has inspired a wide array of authors, games, and films.

98. A. The Overlook Hotel

The Overlook Hotel, the eerie setting of Stephen King's *The Shining*, is inspired by The Stanley Hotel in Colorado. The Overlook's isolation and malevolent forces create a perfect storm for the unraveling of Jack Torrance, making it one of the most memorable locations in horror fiction.

99. False

While *Dracula* is one of the most famous vampire novels, it was preceded by works like John Polidori's *The Vampyre* (1819) and Sheridan Le Fanu's *Carmilla* (1872). Stoker's *Dracula*, however, defined much of the modern vampire mythos and remains a cornerstone of Gothic horror.

100. Shirley Jackson

Shirley Jackson's short story *The Lottery* was first published in 1948 and shocked readers with its depiction of a seemingly ordinary town that engages in a brutal annual ritual. The story critiques conformity and societal violence, cementing Jackson as a master of psychological horror.

QUIZ

101. Which horror film franchise features a possessed doll named Annabelle?

    A. Child's Play
    B. The Conjuring
    C. The Exorcist
    D. Poltergeist

102. True or False: The "Mothman" sightings were first reported in Transylvania in the 1800s.

103. The phrase "Do you like scary movies?" is a famous line from the movie _____.

104. Which horror author wrote *I Am Legend*, a story that inspired several films, including *The Omega Man* and *I Am Legend*?

    A. Stephen King
    B. Richard Matheson
    C. Dean Koontz
    D. Peter Straub

105. True or False: Clive Barker's *Hellraiser* is based on his novella *The Hellbound Heart*.

106. *The Haunting of Hill House*, one of the most acclaimed ghost stories, was written by _____.

ANSWERS

101. B. *The Conjuring*

Annabelle is a recurring character in *The Conjuring* Universe, inspired by real-life paranormal cases investigated by Ed and Lorraine Warren. The haunted doll first appeared in *The Conjuring* (2013) and later starred in her own film series, further solidifying her status as a modern horror icon.

102. False

Nice try, Dracula. The first Mothman sightings occurred in Point Pleasant, West Virginia, in 1966. He's more cornfields and country roads than castles and garlic.

103. *Scream*

Wes Craven's *Scream* (1996) revitalized the slasher genre with its meta-humor and clever twists. The opening scene, featuring the masked Ghostface killer asking "Do you like scary movies?" over the phone, is one of the most memorable in horror film history.

104. B. Richard Matheson

Richard Matheson's *I Am Legend* (1954) is a groundbreaking post-apocalyptic novel about the last man on Earth battling vampiric creatures. The story explores themes of isolation and the nature of humanity. Matheson's influence extends beyond literature, as his work inspired numerous films, including *The Twilight Zone* episodes he wrote.

105. True

Clive Barker's novella *The Hellbound Heart* introduced readers to the sadistic Cenobites and their leader, Pinhead. Barker adapted the story into the 1987 film *Hellraiser*, which became a cult classic and launched a franchise. His unique blend of horror and dark fantasy has made him a legend in the genre.

106. Shirley Jackson

Shirley Jackson's *The Haunting of Hill House* (1959) is a masterpiece of psychological horror. The novel follows a group of people investigating a haunted mansion, blending supernatural elements with deep psychological tension. It has been adapted into films and a critically acclaimed Netflix series.

QUIZ

107. Which of the following movies was based on a novella by Tim Lebbon?

    A. The Silence
    B. Bird Box
    C. A Quiet Place
    D. The Mist

108. In *Dracula*, what is the name of the ship that brings the Count to England?

    A. The Carpathia
    B. The Demeter
    C. The Hesperus
    D. The Mariner

109. True or False: The short story *The Monkey's Paw* features a cursed artifact that grants wishes with tragic consequences.

110. *The Silence of the Lambs* introduced the iconic serial killer _____.

111. What horror franchise features the recurring character Sidney Prescott?

    A. Friday the 13th
    B. Halloween
    C. Scream
    D. The Texas Chainsaw Massacre

112. True or False: The original *Nightmare on Elm Street* was inspired by real events.

ANSWERS

107. A. The Silence

Tim Lebbon's novella *The Silence* was adapted into a Netflix film in 2019. The story follows a family trying to survive in a world overrun by deadly, sound-sensitive creatures. Lebbon, an acclaimed horror and dark fantasy author, is also known for his work on novelizations, tie-ins, and original fiction that often explores themes of survival, fear, and the supernatural.

108. B. The Demeter

In Bram Stoker's *Dracula*, the Count travels to England aboard the ship *The Demeter*. The voyage ends in horror when the ship runs aground with no crew left alive, setting the stage for Dracula's reign of terror. The chilling imagery of the ghost ship has become an iconic moment in Gothic fiction.

109. True

W.W. Jacobs' *The Monkey's Paw* is a classic horror tale about the dangers of tampering with fate. The cursed paw grants three wishes, but each comes with a horrifying cost. Its themes of greed and unintended consequences have made it a staple of horror anthologies.

110. Hannibal Lecter

Thomas Harris' *The Silence of the Lambs* introduced Hannibal Lecter, a brilliant psychiatrist and cannibalistic serial killer. The character became a cultural icon through Anthony Hopkins' chilling portrayal in the 1991 film adaptation, which remains one of the most celebrated thrillers of all time.

111. C. Scream

Sidney Prescott, portrayed by Neve Campbell, is the protagonist of the *Scream* series. Her battles against the masked Ghostface killer have become iconic in horror cinema, blending suspense with self-aware humor. The franchise continues to be a major influence on the genre.

112. True

Wes Craven's *Nightmare on Elm Street* (1984) was partially inspired by articles about young men who died in their sleep after experiencing terrifying nightmares. Craven's creation of Freddy Krueger, a dream-stalking killer, capitalized on the universal fear of vulnerability while sleeping.

QUIZ

113. The phrase "Here's Johnny!" is a famous line from the movie _____.

114. True or False: The Castle of Good Hope in Cape Town is rumored to be one of the most haunted places in South Africa.

115. Which horror author famously said, "We make up horrors to help us cope with the real ones"?

    A. Stephen King
    B. H.P. Lovecraft
    C. Anne Rice
    D. Clive Barker

116. The local Quechua people call Machu Picchu the "Lost City of the _____."

117. True or False: The Roswell Incident of 1947 involved a crashed weather balloon.

ANSWERS

113. *The Shining*

Jack Nicholson's ad-libbed line "Here's Johnny!" in Stanley Kubrick's *The Shining* (1980) is one of the most memorable moments in horror cinema. The scene, where Nicholson's character breaks through a door with an axe, has become a cultural touchstone for terror and madness.

114. *True*

The Castle of Good Hope, built in the 17th century, is a historic fortress and a hotspot for ghostly activity. Visitors report sightings of the "Grey Lady," phantom footsteps, and a ghostly soldier pacing the battlements. These tales make the Castle of Good Hope a must-visit for paranormal fans.

115. *A. Stephen King*

Stephen King, often called the "King of Horror," has written over 60 novels and hundreds of short stories that delve into human fears and supernatural terror. His quote reflects the psychological appeal of horror: it allows readers to confront their anxieties in a safe, imaginative space. Works like *IT*, *The Shining*, and *Carrie* continue to resonate with audiences worldwide.

116. *Dead*

Though commonly referred to as the "Lost City of the Incas," some local legends refer to it as the "Lost City of the Dead" due to the number of tombs and sacrificial practices linked to the site. This name reflects the deep spiritual significance and darker rituals associated with Machu Picchu.

117. *True*

In 1947, a mysterious object crashed near Roswell, New Mexico, sparking widespread speculation about UFOs. The U.S. military initially reported recovering a "flying disc" but later stated it was a weather balloon from a classified project. The incident fueled decades of conspiracy theories about alien cover-ups and inspired countless works of science fiction, cementing Roswell's place in UFO lore.

QUIZ

118. True or False: Silvia Moreno-Garcia's *Mexican Gothic* won the Bram Stoker Award for Superior Achievement in a Novel.

119. *Psycho* by Alfred Hitchcock was inspired by the real-life crimes of _____.

120. What is the name of the mansion so famously written about by author Shirley Jackson?

   A. Hill House
   B. Bly Manor
   C. Crain House
   D. Thornfield Hall

121. What social media app has popularized "ghost hunting" with AR filters that claim to detect paranormal entities?

   A. Snapchat
   B. Instagram
   C. TikTok
   D. Facebook

122. True or False: The Amityville Horror house is located in New Jersey.

123. In *The Ring*, what must one do to break the curse of the haunted videotape?

   A. Destroy all copies of the tape
   B. Solve the tape's hidden puzzle
   C. Make a copy and show it to someone else
   D. Perform a ritual at a haunted well

ANSWERS

118. True

Silvia Moreno-Garcia's *Mexican Gothic* captivated readers with its gothic atmosphere and rich cultural backdrop. Set in 1950s Mexico, the novel reinvents traditional gothic tropes while exploring themes of colonialism, family secrets, and horror within the confines of a decaying mansion.

119. Ed Gein

Ed Gein, a notorious murderer and body snatcher from Wisconsin, served as the chilling inspiration for characters like Norman Bates in *Psycho*, Leatherface in *The Texas Chainsaw Massacre*, and Buffalo Bill in *The Silence of the Lambs*. His gruesome crimes, including crafting items from human remains, shocked the nation and left an indelible mark on the horror genre.

120. A. Hill House

Shirley Jackson's *The Haunting of Hill House* features Hill House as the central, malevolent character. The mansion's eerie presence affects everyone who enters, creating a tense and haunting atmosphere. Considered one of the best ghost stories ever written, it has inspired multiple adaptations, including a Netflix series.

121. A. Snapchat

Snapchat's AR filters, originally designed for fun overlays, have been used by users to "hunt ghosts." Some filters appear to detect faces or movements in empty rooms, sparking creepy videos and debates about whether these interactions are glitches or genuine paranormal phenomena.

122. False. It's located in New York.

The Amityville Horror house, located in Amityville, New York, gained notoriety after the Lutz family claimed they experienced paranormal activity following a gruesome murder in the home. In 1974, Ronald DeFeo Jr. killed six members of his family there. The subsequent hauntings became the basis for a bestselling book and a film franchise, though skeptics question the authenticity of the claims.

123. C. Make a copy and show it to someone else

The American remake of the Japanese film *Ringu*, *The Ring* centers on a cursed videotape that kills the viewer in seven days unless they copy it and pass it on, creating a chilling chain letter effect.

QUIZ

124. The 1897 horror novel *Dracula* begins with Jonathan Harker traveling to _____.

125. What is the name of the infamous poltergeist case investigated by Ed and Lorraine Warren?

    A. The Perron Family Haunting
    B. The Enfield Poltergeist
    C. The Amityville Horror
    D. The Smurl Haunting

126. True or False: The cursed ship *The Flying Dutchman* has been sighted by sailors for centuries.

127. True or False: A TikTok user known as @itsmarziapie went viral after posting videos of their allegedly haunted apartment, featuring moving furniture and eerie whispers.

128. Which 1898 horror novel takes the form of a series of letters and documents, telling the story of a governess's descent into madness?

    A. The Turn of the Screw
    B. Dracula
    C. The Strange Case of Dr. Jekyll and Mr. Hyde
    D. The Picture of Dorian Gray

129. True or False: The Salem Witch Trials resulted in the execution of over 100 people.

ANSWERS

124. Transylvania

In Bram Stoker's *Dracula*, Jonathan Harker journeys to Transylvania to assist Count Dracula with a real estate transaction. Unbeknownst to Harker, Dracula plans to spread his vampiric curse to England. The novel's vivid descriptions of the Carpathian Mountains and Dracula's eerie castle have captivated readers for over a century, defining the modern vampire mythos.

125. B. The Enfield Poltergeist

The Enfield Poltergeist case occurred in the late 1970s in England, involving a family who reported violent paranormal activity, including furniture moving and disembodied voices. Ed and Lorraine Warren, renowned paranormal investigators, documented the events, which inspired *The Conjuring 2*. While skeptics dismissed it as a hoax, the case remains one of the most famous in paranormal history.

126. True

The legend of *The Flying Dutchman* tells of a ghostly ship doomed to sail the seas forever. First reported in the 17th century, the vessel is often seen glowing in the distance, a harbinger of doom for sailors. Stories of the ship have appeared in numerous literary works and films, including the *Pirates of the Caribbean* series.

127. True

@itsmarziapie's TikToks showcase unexplained events, such as cabinets slamming shut, furniture moving on its own, and strange whispers caught on audio. The videos sparked debates, with some viewers convinced it was a genuine haunting and others suspecting clever special effects.

128. The Turn of the Screw

Henry James's *The Turn of the Screw* is a psychological horror novella that uses an epistolary format to tell the unsettling story of a governess caring for two children at a remote estate. The tale's ambiguity—whether the ghosts she sees are real or figments of her imagination—has sparked debate for over a century, making it a cornerstone of Gothic fiction.

129. False. 20 people were executed.

The Salem Witch Trials of 1692 led to the execution of 20 individuals—14 women and 6 men—accused of witchcraft in colonial Massachusetts. While hundreds were accused and imprisoned, the trials ended before the death toll could climb higher. This dark chapter in history highlights the dangers of mass hysteria and unfounded accusations.

QUIZ

130. The 1973 film *The Exorcist* was based on a novel by _____.

131. What type of spider served as the "villain" in the 1990 horror-comedy *Arachnophobia*?

    A. A tarantula
    B. A deadly hybrid spider
    C. A wolf spider
    D. A black widow

132. What cryptid is said to inhabit the Pine Barrens of New Jersey?

    A. The Mothman
    B. The Jersey Devil
    C. The Chupacabra
    D. The Thunderbird

133. What Instagram user went viral for posting a series of photos showing their reflection acting independently in mirrors?

    A. @HauntedReflections
    B. @ShadowGlass
    C. @SpectralSelfies
    D. @PhantomFrames

134. True or False: Edgar Allan Poe's *The Raven* was inspired by his obsession with death and loss.

135. The Dyatlov Pass incident of 1959 involved the mysterious deaths of (how many) _____ hikers in the Ural Mountains.

ANSWERS

130. William Peter Blatty

William Peter Blatty's *The Exorcist* was inspired by a 1949 case of demonic possession. The novel's adaptation into a film shocked audiences with its graphic depictions of possession and exorcism, earning it the reputation of one of the scariest movies of all time. Blatty's work remains a defining piece of horror fiction.

131. B. A deadly hybrid spider

In *Arachnophobia*, the antagonist is a fictional hybrid spider created when a deadly South American spider mates with a common house spider. This hybrid becomes highly venomous and spreads terror in a small American town. The film, blending horror and comedy, became a cult classic for its ability to make even the most harmless spiders seem terrifying.

132. B. The Jersey Devil

The Jersey Devil is a legendary creature said to haunt the Pine Barrens of New Jersey. Described as having a goat-like head, bat wings, and a forked tail, it has been the subject of folklore since the 18th century. While skeptics dismiss sightings as hoaxes or misidentifications, the Jersey Devil remains an enduring figure in American cryptozoology.

133. A. @HauntedReflections

@HauntedReflections shared unsettling photos where their mirror reflection appeared to be looking in a different direction or smiling when they weren't. The posts sparked debates about optical illusions, Photoshop, or potential supernatural activity.

134. True

Edgar Allan Poe's *The Raven*, published in 1845, is a dark and melancholic poem that explores themes of grief and despair. The narrator, mourning the loss of his beloved Lenore, is visited by a mysterious raven that repeats the word "Nevermore." Poe's fascination with death and the macabre made this poem an enduring symbol of Gothic literature.

135. Nine

The Dyatlov Pass incident remains one of history's most chilling unsolved mysteries. Nine experienced hikers died under bizarre circumstances in the Ural Mountains, with some found shoeless and others with unexplained injuries, such as fractured skulls and missing tongues. Theories range from avalanches and military experiments to UFOs and yetis, but no conclusive explanation has ever been found.

QUIZ

136. What is the name of the 1981 horror film where a group of friends is terrorized by demonic forces in a remote cabin?

   A. The Evil Dead
   B. The Texas Chainsaw Massacre
   C. Friday the 13th
   D. Halloween

137. True or False: H.P. Lovecraft lived to see his work achieve widespread acclaim.

138. What is the name of the French chateau infamous for its connection to the murders of Gilles de Rais, a 15th-century nobleman and alleged serial killer?

   A. Château de Brissac
   B. Château de Tiffauges
   C. Château de Versailles
   D. Château d'If

139. True or False: The book *Dracula* was banned in Ireland when it was first published.

140. What unusual location does the group in *Bird Box* decide to travel to in order to escape the entities?

   A. An abandoned hospital
   B. A secluded monastery
   C. A sanctuary for the blind
   D. A heavily guarded military base

141. True or False: A Reddit user in 2018 shared photos of what they believed to be a ghost in their home, captured using a motion-activated pet camera.

ANSWERS

136. A. The Evil Dead

Sam Raimi's *The Evil Dead* became a cult classic, known for its gruesome special effects and innovative camera work. The film's low budget didn't stop it from becoming one of the most influential horror movies of all time, spawning sequels, a television series, and a devoted fanbase.

137. False

H.P. Lovecraft, the creator of the Cthulhu Mythos, died in 1937 in relative obscurity. His work, which explores cosmic horror and humanity's insignificance in the universe, gained popularity posthumously. Today, Lovecraft is considered one of the most influential horror writers of all time, with his stories inspiring generations of authors and creators.

138. B. Château de Tiffauges

Gilles de Rais, a wealthy nobleman and former military commander, is believed to have murdered hundreds of children in the 15th century. His crimes were allegedly committed at Château de Tiffauges, earning it the nickname "Castle of Horror." De Rais' dark history inspired legends and may have contributed to the tale of *Bluebeard*, the murderous nobleman in French folklore.

139. False

Bram Stoker's *Dracula* was published in 1897, and while it stirred the pot of gothic horror, it was never officially banned in his homeland. In fact, some believe it reflects Stoker's anxieties about British colonialism and repressed sexuality more than religious outrage.

140. C. A sanctuary for the blind

In *Bird Box*, the group seeks safety at a community of blind individuals, as the entities cannot affect those who cannot see. This clever twist highlights the importance of the blindfolds and emphasizes the creative world-building that makes the story so compelling.

141. True

The photos showed a translucent figure moving through the living room, prompting debates on r/GhostStories. Some believed it was a genuine haunting, while others suggested glitches or reflections. The user claimed their pets started acting strangely after the sightings, adding to the eerie vibe.

142. True or False: The Winchester Mystery House was constructed with no architectural plans, leading to its bizarre and labyrinthine design.

143. The unsolved mystery of the _____ colony, established in 1587, is marked by the disappearance of its settlers, with the word "CROATOAN" left behind as a clue.

144. What is the name of the ghost town in Nevada known for its haunted bottle house and eerie atmosphere?

   A. Bodie
   B. Rhyolite
   C. Virginia City
   D. Goldfield

145. True or False: The island of Poveglia in Italy was used as a quarantine station and later as a mental asylum.

146. The infamous Bloody Mary legend involves summoning her spirit by chanting her name in front of a _____.

ANSWERS

142. *True*

The Winchester Mystery House in San Jose, California, was continuously constructed for 38 years by Sarah Winchester, heiress to the Winchester rifle fortune. Believing she was haunted by the spirits of those killed by her family's rifles, she built the mansion to confuse the ghosts. The house includes staircases to nowhere, doors that open into walls, and over 160 rooms, cementing its reputation as one of the most haunted places in America.

143. *Roanoke*

The Roanoke Colony, established on Roanoke Island in modern-day North Carolina, vanished without a trace by 1590. The only clue was the word "CROATOAN" carved into a post. Theories about the settlers' fate range from assimilation with Native tribes to alien abduction or even supernatural causes. The mystery of Roanoke remains one of early America's most enduring enigmas.

144. *B. Rhyolite*

Rhyolite, a ghost town in Nevada, flourished during the early 1900s gold rush but was abandoned by 1920 after the mines failed. Among its remnants is the haunted bottle house, constructed from glass bottles. Visitors have reported ghostly figures and strange noises, making Rhyolite a chilling destination for paranormal enthusiasts.

145. *True*

Poveglia, a small island near Venice, is one of the world's most haunted locations. During the Black Death, it served as a quarantine station where thousands of plague victims were sent to die. Later, it became a mental asylum where patients reportedly endured cruel experiments. Poveglia is now abandoned, with locals claiming it is cursed and haunted by restless spirits.

146. *Mirror*

The Bloody Mary legend is a popular urban myth involving the summoning of a ghostly figure by chanting "Bloody Mary" three times in front of a mirror, usually in a dark room. Variations of the legend suggest she appears to reveal your future or as a vengeful spirit. Though rooted in folklore, the ritual remains a spooky party game and a source of nightmares.

QUIZ

147. Which actor appeared in *Paranormal Activity 2* before going on to star in the hit TV show *Yellowstone*?

    A. Luke Grimes
    B. Josh Lucas
    C. David Oyelowo
    D. Brian Boland

148. True or False: The Tower of London is haunted by the ghost of Anne Boleyn, who was executed there in 1536.

149. What is the name of the woman found dead in Oslo's Plaza Hotel in 1995, whose identity remains unknown?

    A. The Isdal Woman
    B. The Plaza Woman
    C. The Lady in Red
    D. The Somerton Woman

150. What mysterious feature of Machu Picchu's architecture has led to speculation about its otherworldly origins?

    A. Its alignment with celestial constellations
    B. The magnetic properties of the stones
    C. Hidden chambers beneath the site
    D. Symbols resembling alien glyphs

151. True or False: The disappearance of Amelia Earhart and her navigator, Fred Noonan, was definitively solved in 2018.

ANSWERS

147. D. Brian Boland

Brian Boland played Daniel Rey, the sceptical husband in *Paranormal Activity 2*. He later popped up in multiple film and TV projects, including *Yellowstone*. Apparently, terror prepares you for cattle ranch drama.

148. True

The Tower of London, with its grim history of executions and imprisonment, is one of the most haunted places in England. Anne Boleyn, the ill-fated wife of Henry VIII, was executed on its grounds, and her ghost is said to wander the tower, sometimes carrying her severed head. Numerous other spirits are rumored to haunt the site, adding to its chilling allure.

149. B. The Plaza Woman

Dubbed "The Plaza Woman," this unidentified woman checked into the Oslo Plaza Hotel under a false name. She was later found dead in her room with no ID or personal belongings. Despite investigations, her identity and the circumstances of her death remain a mystery, making it one of Norway's most puzzling cold cases.

150. A. Its alignment with celestial constellations

Machu Picchu's structures align perfectly with astronomical events like solstices and equinoxes, leading some to theorize that the Incas had otherworldly knowledge or assistance. While this is likely a testament to their advanced understanding of astronomy, the precision still fuels speculation.

151. False

Amelia Earhart and Fred Noonan vanished in 1937 while attempting to circumnavigate the globe. Their plane disappeared over the Pacific, sparking decades of speculation. Theories range from a crash at sea to Earhart living secretly under another identity. While artifacts and bones have been found on Nikumaroro Island, conclusive evidence remains elusive.

152. The unsolved case of the Zodiac Killer involved letters and ciphers sent to _____.

153. What is the name of the Australian cold case involving an unidentified man found dead on a beach in 1948?

    A. The Beaumont Mystery
    B. The Somerton Man
    C. The Tamam Shud Case
    D. Both B and C

154. True or False: The Dyatlov Pass incident involved the discovery of hikers with radiation on their clothing.

155. The disappearance of three young siblings in 1966 from a beach in Adelaide, Australia, is known as the _____ Mystery.

156. True or False: Bill Skarsgård's portrayal of Pennywise in the 2017 film included a real drooping eye effect achieved without CGI.

157. A YouTube channel called *The Backrooms Explorer* documents eerie videos of endless, labyrinth-like _____.

ANSWERS

152. *Newspapers*

The Zodiac Killer terrorized California in the late 1960s, claiming responsibility for multiple murders. The killer taunted authorities by sending letters and cryptic ciphers to local newspapers. Despite extensive investigations and potential suspects, the Zodiac Killer's identity remains unknown, making it one of the most infamous unsolved cases in history.

153. *D. Both B and C*

The Somerton Man, also known as the Tamam Shud Case, is an enduring mystery. Found dead on Somerton Beach in Adelaide, Australia, the man carried no identification, and a scrap of paper reading "Tamam Shud" (meaning "ended" in Persian) was found in his pocket. Despite extensive efforts, his identity and cause of death remain unknown, leading to theories of espionage and murder.

154. *True*

In 1959, nine hikers died under mysterious circumstances in the Ural Mountains. Some of their bodies exhibited unexplained injuries, and traces of radiation were found on their clothing. Theories include avalanches, military testing, and even UFOs, but the truth behind the Dyatlov Pass incident remains a chilling enigma.

155. *Beaumont Children*

The Beaumont Children vanished from Glenelg Beach on Australia Day in 1966, sparking one of the largest searches in the country's history. Despite numerous leads and suspects, no trace of the children has ever been found. Their disappearance remains one of Australia's most haunting unsolved cases.

156. *True*

Bill Skarsgård's Pennywise is unnerving partly due to his physicality, including his ability to make one eye droop independently. Skarsgård used this unique skill to enhance Pennywise's creepy, inhuman appearance, adding to the film's unsettling atmosphere.

157. *Hallways*

The *Backrooms Explorer* channel expanded on the viral concept of "The Backrooms," an urban legend about liminal spaces with endless, eerie hallways. The videos feature unsettling noises, flickering lights, and a growing sense of dread, captivating fans of internet horror.

QUIZ

158. Which *"A Nightmare on Elm Street"* actor made his film debut in the franchise before becoming a global superstar?

    A. Brad Pitt
    B. Keanu Reeves
    C. Johnny Depp
    D. Leonardo DiCaprio

159. What prestigious award is presented annually by the Horror Writers Association (HWA)?

    A. The Bram Stoker Award
    B. The Shirley Jackson Prize
    C. The Edgar Allan Poe Medal
    D. The Stephen King Trophy

160. True or False: The "Boy in the Box" case was solved in 2022.

161. Which real-life murders inspired Truman Capote's *In Cold Blood*, one of the first nonfiction novels?

    A. The Villisca Axe Murders
    B. The Black Dahlia Case
    C. The Clutter Family Murders
    D. The JonBenét Ramsey Case

162. What is the title of John Connolly's debut novel that introduced his iconic detective Charlie Parker and blended crime fiction with supernatural elements?

    A. The Killing Kind
    B. The Book of Lost Things
    C. Every Dead Thing
    D. The Whisperers

163. True or False: The novel *Jaws* by Peter Benchley was inspired by real shark attacks along the New Jersey coast in 1916.

158. C. Johnny Depp

In *A Nightmare on Elm Street* (1984), Depp gets pulled into a bed and turned into a geyser of blood. It's his very first film role, and Freddy Krueger made sure it was unforgettable.

159. A. The Bram Stoker Award

The Horror Writers Association presents the Bram Stoker Award annually to recognize superior achievement in horror writing. Named after the author of *Dracula*, the award celebrates works in various categories, including novels, short stories, and screenplays, and has become one of the most coveted honors in the genre. Crystal Lake Publishing, the publisher of the very book you're holding now, is a recipient of the HWA's Specialty Press Award.

160. False

The "Boy in the Box" case involves the 1957 discovery of an unidentified boy's body in Philadelphia. Known as "America's Unknown Child," the boy was found in a cardboard box, and his death remains a mystery. Despite modern advances in forensic technology, his identity and the circumstances of his death have yet to be determined.

161. C. The Clutter Family Murders

In 1959, the Clutter family was brutally murdered in their Kansas farmhouse, shocking the nation. Truman Capote extensively researched the case and the killers, crafting *In Cold Blood*, a groundbreaking true-crime novel. The book's meticulous detail and narrative style redefined the genre, blending fact and fiction to chilling effect.

162. C. Every Dead Thing

John Connolly's debut novel *Every Dead Thing* (1999) introduced Charlie Parker, a private detective haunted by the brutal murder of his wife and child. The novel's seamless blend of crime fiction and supernatural horror set it apart, establishing Connolly as a master of dark, atmospheric storytelling.

163. True

The 1916 Jersey Shore shark attacks involved multiple fatalities over two weeks, causing widespread panic. These events, combined with scientific misunderstandings of shark behavior, inspired Peter Benchley's *Jaws*. The novel and its 1975 film adaptation heightened fears of sharks but also led to increased efforts in shark conservation.

QUIZ

164. Which coveted literary award was replaced in 2015 due to controversies surrounding its design?

    A. The Bram Stoker Award
    B. The Shirley Jackson Award
    C. The World Fantasy Award
    D. The Nebula Award

165. The gruesome crimes of _____ inspired the characters of Norman Bates, Leatherface, and Buffalo Bill.

166. What Egyptian pharaoh was believed to have reigned as a woman, often depicted with a false beard?

    A. Cleopatra VII
    B. Nefertiti
    C. Hatshepsut
    D. Sobekneferu

167. What notorious 19th-century murder inspired Mary Shelley's *Frankenstein*?

    A. The Ratcliffe Highway Murders
    B. The Burke and Hare Killings
    C. The Galvanism Experiments on George Forster
    D. The Murder of William Weare

168. True or False: Stephen King's *Carrie* was inspired by a real-life case of bullying that ended in tragedy.

169. The Salem Witch Trials of _____ (year) inspired Arthur Miller's play *The Crucible*.

ANSWERS

164. C. The World Fantasy Award

The World Fantasy Award previously featured a bust of H.P. Lovecraft, designed by Gahan Wilson. However, due to controversies surrounding Lovecraft's views on race, the design was replaced in 2015 with a more neutral sculpture. Despite the change, the award continues to celebrate excellence in speculative fiction.

165. Ed Gein

Ed Gein, a murderer and grave robber from Wisconsin, shocked the nation when authorities discovered he had crafted household items from human remains. His macabre crimes influenced iconic horror characters, including Norman Bates in *Psycho*, Leatherface in *The Texas Chainsaw Massacre*, and Buffalo Bill in *The Silence of the Lambs*. Gein's dark legacy remains a key reference in horror history.

166. C. Hatshepsut

Hatshepsut, one of ancient Egypt's most successful pharaohs, ruled during the 18th Dynasty and was often depicted wearing a false beard to assert her authority. Her reign was marked by prosperity and monumental building projects, but after her death, efforts were made to erase her legacy from history.

167. C. The Galvanism Experiments on George Forster

The case of George Forster, executed in 1803, inspired debates on galvanism—the use of electricity to reanimate dead tissue. Public demonstrations of galvanism on his corpse fascinated Mary Shelley, influencing the creation of Dr. Frankenstein and his creature. This merging of science and horror in *Frankenstein* became a hallmark of Gothic fiction.

168. True

Stephen King drew inspiration for *Carrie* from two girls he knew in high school who were outcasts and suffered relentless bullying. Though neither story ended in supernatural revenge, King used their experiences to create a tale of telekinetic vengeance, turning *Carrie* into one of the most iconic horror novels of all time.

169. 1692

Arthur Miller wrote *The Crucible* during the 1950s as an allegory for McCarthyism, using the Salem Witch Trials as a parallel to the Red Scare. The hysteria, false accusations, and devastating consequences of both events made Miller's work a timeless exploration of paranoia and injustice.

QUIZ

170. What real-life event inspired Daphne du Maurier's short story "The Birds"?

    A. A mass bird migration in California
    B. A toxic algae bloom causing birds to attack humans
    C. A series of bird strikes on airplanes in the 1940s
    D. None of the above

171. What is the name of Joe Mynhardt's series of books aimed at helping authors with branding, marketing, and the craft of writing?

    A. The Author's Toolkit
    B. Shadows & Ink
    C. The Writer's Forge
    D. Horror & Beyond

172. True or False: The unsolved Black Dahlia murder inspired the novel and film *L.A. Confidential.*

173. What real-life paranormal investigation inspired the 2013 film *The Conjuring*?

    A. The Enfield Poltergeist
    B. The Perron Family Haunting
    C. The Amityville Horror
    D. The Smurl Haunting

174. What significant contribution did Rocky Wood, a former president of the Horror Writers Association (HWA), make to the study of Stephen King's work?

    A. He wrote the first authorized biography of Stephen King.
    B. He co-authored several novels with King.
    C. He compiled an exhaustive guide to King's unpublished and uncollected works.
    D. He directed a documentary on King's life.

ANSWERS

170. B. A toxic algae bloom causing birds to attack humans

In 1961, residents of Capitola, California, reported aggressive bird behavior, including birds flying into windows and attacking people. Scientists later linked the event to a toxic algae bloom affecting the birds' behavior. Daphne du Maurier's eerie story, later adapted into Alfred Hitchcock's film *The Birds*, was influenced by this strange occurrence.

171. B. Shadows & Ink

Joe Mynhardt's *Shadows & Ink* series provides authors with essential tools and insights for branding, marketing, and mastering their craft. Geared toward speculative fiction and horror writers, the series blends practical strategies with inspiration, making it a go-to resource for navigating the publishing world.

172. True

The Black Dahlia murder, involving the gruesome death of aspiring actress Elizabeth Short in 1947, has remained one of Hollywood's most infamous cold cases. While *L.A. Confidential* is fictional, it incorporates themes of corruption and murder tied to the glitzy but dark underbelly of 1940s Los Angeles, echoing the haunting legacy of the Black Dahlia case.

173. B. The Perron Family Haunting

The Perron family moved into a farmhouse in Rhode Island in the 1970s and claimed to experience terrifying paranormal activity, including malevolent spirits. Paranormal investigators Ed and Lorraine Warren documented the case, which became the basis for *The Conjuring*. The film's success launched a franchise exploring other cases investigated by the Warrens.

174. C. He compiled an exhaustive guide to King's unpublished and uncollected works.

Rocky Wood, HWA president from 2010 to 2014, was renowned for his scholarship on Stephen King's writing. His works, such as *Stephen King: Uncollected, Unpublished*, offered unparalleled insights into King's lesser-known pieces and drafts. Wood was deeply respected for his dedication to the genre, both as a researcher and an advocate for horror writers worldwide. Despite battling ALS, he continued to contribute to the horror community until his passing in 2014, leaving behind a legacy of passion and scholarship.

QUIZ

175. The 1976 film *The Town That Dreaded Sundown* was based on a series of murders committed by _____, an unidentified killer in Texarkana, Arkansas.

176. The so-called "Curse of the _____" is associated with opening ancient Egyptian tombs.

177. Which movie was inspired by a real-life story of a possessed boy, later adapted into a famous 1973 horror film?

   A. The Omen
   B. The Exorcist
   C. Poltergeist
   D. Rosemary's Baby

178. The 2008 film *The Strangers* was inspired by a series of break-ins committed by _____.

179. Which movie is based on the story of George and Kathy Lutz, who fled their home claiming it was haunted by malevolent forces?

   A. The Amityville Horror
   B. Poltergeist
   C. The Haunting
   D. Hereditary

180. True or False: The 1999 movie *The Blair Witch Project* was based on a real documentary about missing hikers in Maryland.

ANSWERS

175. *The Phantom Killer*

The Phantom Killer terrorized Texarkana in 1946, attacking couples in secluded areas and leaving five people dead. The case remains unsolved, and the killer's identity is unknown. The film *The Town That Dreaded Sundown* dramatized these events, blending fact and fiction to create an enduring urban legend.

176. *Pharaohs*

The "Curse of the Pharaohs" is a popular myth suggesting that anyone who disturbs a pharaoh's tomb will face misfortune or death. While often dismissed as superstition, the deaths of several individuals connected to the discovery of King Tutankhamun's tomb in the 1920s fueled the legend.

177. *B. The Exorcist*

The Exorcist is based on a 1949 exorcism performed on a boy known by the pseudonym "Roland Doe." The case involved violent outbursts, unexplainable phenomena, and the boy speaking in foreign languages. William Peter Blatty's novel and its film adaptation brought the story into popular culture, terrifying audiences worldwide.

178. *The Keddie Cabin Murderers*

While loosely based on true events, *The Strangers* drew inspiration from the Keddie Cabin Murders in 1981, where four people were brutally killed in a remote cabin. The film's unsettling premise of strangers targeting a couple at their home taps into primal fears of vulnerability and random violence.

179. *A. The Amityville Horror*

The Lutz family's claims of paranormal activity in their home at 112 Ocean Avenue, following the murders of the DeFeo family, became the basis for *The Amityville Horror*. Though skeptics question their story, the book and film adaptation became cultural phenomena, spawning sequels and debates about the reality of hauntings.

180. *False*

While *The Blair Witch Project* was marketed as found footage of a real investigation, it is entirely fictional. The film's creators fabricated the story of the Blair Witch and used clever marketing to convince audiences it was real, revolutionizing the found-footage genre and creating a new approach to horror storytelling.

QUIZ

181. What nickname did Jamie Lee Curtis earn after starring in a series of successful horror films in the late 1970s and early 1980s?

    A. The Queen of Screams
    B. The First Lady of Fear
    C. The Scream Queen
    D. The Horror Heroine

182. The 1932 disappearance of Australian farmer Harold Holt during a _____ remains an enduring mystery.

183. What 19th-century artifact was found buried under a London river and linked to multiple deaths of those who uncovered it?

    A. The London Mummy
    B. The Unlucky Pharaoh's Curse
    C. The Hexham Heads
    D. The Battersea Shield

184. The Great Fire of _____ destroyed a significant portion of the city in 1666 but also helped end a devastating plague.

185. Which horror icon is Tony Todd best known for portraying?

    A. The Tall Man
    B. The Djinn
    C. The Creeper
    D. Candyman

186. What unexplained series of murders in 1946 left Texarkana residents terrified, inspiring the nickname "The Moonlight Murders"?

    A. The Phantom Killer
    B. The Zodiac Murders
    C. The Midnight Stalker
    D. The Shadow Slayer

ANSWERS

181. C. The Scream Queen

Jamie Lee Curtis earned the title of *The Scream Queen* for her iconic performances in horror classics like *Halloween* (1978), *The Fog* (1980), and *Prom Night* (1980). Her portrayal of Laurie Strode in *Halloween* cemented her status as a horror legend, and she has reprised the role in several sequels, most recently in the 2018 revival and its follow-ups.

182. Swimming expedition

Australian Prime Minister Harold Holt disappeared while swimming off the coast of Victoria in 1967, sparking countless conspiracy theories. From drowning to alien abduction, the mystery of Holt's disappearance remains unsolved, cementing his case as one of Australia's strangest political enigmas.

183. D. The Battersea Shield

The Battersea Shield, an intricately designed Iron Age artifact, was discovered in the River Thames in 1857. While it is primarily a historical treasure, local legends claim it brought misfortune to those involved in its recovery, leading to whispers of a curse. Its true history, however, remains mysterious.

184. London

The Great Fire of London raged for four days, destroying much of the city's wooden structures. Though catastrophic, the fire also eradicated many of the rats and unsanitary conditions that had fueled the bubonic plague, inadvertently bringing an end to the epidemic. The event marked a turning point in urban redevelopment.

185. D. Candyman

Tony Todd terrified audiences with his haunting performance in *Candyman* (1992), bringing elegance, tragedy, and menace to the role of the hook-handed specter. His deep voice and commanding presence made him unforgettable—and earned him a place in horror legend.

186. A. The Phantom Killer

The Phantom Killer attacked eight people in Texarkana over several months in 1946, killing five. The murders occurred in secluded areas under the cover of night, sparking fear and curfews. Despite a massive investigation, the case remains unsolved, leaving behind a legacy of fear and speculation.

QUIZ

187. True or False: The cursed Hope Diamond is believed to have caused misfortune and death to many of its owners.

188. What unsolved mystery involved the discovery of mutilated cattle in the American Midwest during the 1970s?

    A. The Skinwalker Ranch Incidents
    B. The Cattle Mutilation Phenomenon
    C. The Dulce Base Conspiracy
    D. The Rancher's Curse

189. Rachel Harrison's debut novel, *The Return*, centers on a group of friends reuniting at a remote _____ after one of them mysteriously disappears.

190. True or False: Some of the stones at Stonehenge were transported over 150 miles from Wales.

191. True or False: South Africa has its own version of the urban legend about "tokoloshes,"small, mischievous supernatural beings.

192. True or False: The Vanishing of the Flannan Isles Lighthouse Keepers in 1900 remains an unsolved mystery.

ANSWERS

187. True

The Hope Diamond, a rare blue diamond weighing over 45 carats, is rumored to be cursed. Stories of its owners facing financial ruin, tragedy, or death have persisted for centuries. Now housed in the Smithsonian Institution, the diamond's dark reputation continues to fascinate and terrify.

188. B. The Cattle Mutilation Phenomenon

The Cattle Mutilation Phenomenon refers to a series of unexplained livestock deaths during the 1970s, where animals were found with precise surgical wounds and missing organs. Theories ranged from alien experiments to secret government programs. Despite investigations, no conclusive explanation has ever been found, adding to the eerie mystery.

189. Hotel

In *The Return*, Rachel Harrison crafts a suspenseful tale of friendship and terror as a woman reappears after being missing for two years, bringing something dark and unknown back with her. Harrison's fresh voice has earned her a spot among rising stars in modern horror.

190. True

The smaller "bluestones" at Stonehenge were sourced from the Preseli Hills in Wales, over 150 miles away. The logistics of moving these massive stones during the Neolithic period remain a marvel of ancient engineering and have sparked theories about early technology, teamwork, and even supernatural assistance.

191. True

The tokoloshe is a creature from Zulu mythology, described as a small, hairy being capable of causing harm or mischief. It is said to be summoned by witch doctors to frighten or curse individuals. Tokoloshe stories are deeply ingrained in South African culture, blending superstition and folklore.

192. True

In December 1900, three lighthouse keepers disappeared from the remote Flannan Isles off the coast of Scotland. When a relief vessel arrived, the keepers were nowhere to be found, and their logbook contained cryptic entries about storms and strange feelings. Despite numerous theories, from rogue waves to madness, their fate remains unknown.

QUIZ

193. The Dyatlov Pass Incident of 1959 involved mysterious deaths in the _____ Mountains.

194. What bizarre 1845 disappearance involved a doomed Arctic expedition searching for the Northwest Passage?

    A. The Endurance Expedition
    B. The Franklin Expedition
    C. The Shackleton Mission
    D. The Erebus and Terror Journey

195. True or False: The Moberly-Jourdain Incident involved two women claiming to have time-traveled to 18th-century Versailles.

196. What mysterious archaeological site features massive stone heads and remains of an ancient civilization?

    A. Stonehenge
    B. Easter Island
    C. Machu Picchu
    D. Gobekli Tepe

197. What is the name of the mastermind behind the deadly games in the *Saw* franchise?

    A. Jigsaw
    B. Puzzle Master
    C. The Architect
    D. The Collector

198. True or False: The Hinterkaifeck Murders in 1922 Germany involved a family killed on their remote farm by an unknown assailant.

ANSWERS

193. *Ural*

Nine hikers in the Ural Mountains were found dead under bizarre circumstances, including missing tongues and signs of radiation. Theories about the Dyatlov Pass Incident include military testing, avalanches, or even Yeti attacks. The case remains one of history's most chilling unsolved mysteries.

194. *B. The Franklin Expedition*

The Franklin Expedition, led by Sir John Franklin, vanished while attempting to chart the Northwest Passage. The ships, *HMS Erebus* and *HMS Terror*, were trapped in ice, and the crew succumbed to starvation, hypothermia, and possibly lead poisoning or cannibalism. The wrecks were only rediscovered in the 21st century, leaving questions unanswered.

195. *True*

In 1901, two English women, Charlotte Anne Moberly and Eleanor Jourdain, claimed they encountered people and scenes from 18th-century Versailles while visiting the Petit Trianon. The incident, known as a "time slip," sparked debate over whether it was a supernatural event, a shared hallucination, or an elaborate hoax.

196. *B. Easter Island*

Easter Island, or Rapa Nui, is famous for its massive stone statues called moai, carved by the island's Polynesian inhabitants. The purpose of the statues and the reasons behind the civilization's decline remain mysteries, with theories including ecological collapse and overpopulation.

197. *A. Jigsaw*

John Kramer, known as Jigsaw, orchestrates elaborate traps to test his victims' will to live, forcing them to make harrowing choices. The *Saw* series is known for its complex plot and moral dilemmas.

198. *True*

The Hinterkaifeck Murders remain one of Germany's most chilling unsolved cases. Six members of the Gruber family were found brutally murdered with a pickaxe, and signs suggested the killer had lived in their home for days before the crime. Despite extensive investigations, the murderer was never identified.

QUIZ

199. True or False: The Great Pyramid of Giza was originally covered in smooth, white limestone casing stones.

200. True or False: Cleopatra VII was the last pharaoh of ancient Egypt.

201. What ghost is said to haunt a stretch of road in the Karoo, South Africa, appearing to hitchhikers before vanishing?

   A. The Phantom Driver
   B. The Uniondale Hitchhiker
   C. The Lady in White
   D. The Karoo Wanderer

202. What peculiar sound phenomenon is associated with the bluestones of Stonehenge?

   A. They hum when struck.
   B. They amplify nearby voices.
   C. They echo louder than other stones.
   D. They vibrate during solstices.

203. True or False: *Critters* were directly inspired by the success of *Gremlins*.

204. True or False: A Twitter thread in 2017 detailed a user's alleged encounters with a ghostly child named "Dear David."

ANSWERS

199. True

The Great Pyramid of Giza, built for Pharaoh Khufu, was originally covered in polished limestone casing stones, making it gleam brilliantly under the sun. Most of the casing stones were removed over centuries for other construction projects, leaving the stepped core structure visible today. Its original appearance added to its mystical aura.

200. True

Cleopatra VII, part of the Ptolemaic dynasty, was the last active ruler of ancient Egypt. Her dramatic life, alliances with Julius Caesar and Mark Antony, and ultimate defeat by Octavian led to Egypt becoming a Roman province. Cleopatra's legacy endures as one of history's most enigmatic and powerful figures.

201. B. The Uniondale Hitchhiker

The Uniondale Hitchhiker legend tells of a young woman who died in a car crash on Easter weekend in 1968. Drivers on this stretch of road claim to see her hitchhiking; she disappears from the car shortly after being picked up. The chilling story has made this road infamous among ghost enthusiasts.

202. A. They hum when struck.

The bluestones of Stonehenge are known to produce a resonant humming sound when struck, leading some researchers to theorize that they were chosen for their acoustic properties. This has fueled speculation that Stonehenge may have been a site for musical or ritualistic ceremonies.

203. False

While *Critters* was released shortly after *Gremlins* (1984), the script was written before *Gremlins* came out. However, the films share a similar blend of horror and comedy, leading to comparisons. *Critters* stands out for its sci-fi elements and unique alien backstory.

204. True

Writer Adam Ellis posted a series of tweets about a ghostly child he called "Dear David," who allegedly haunted his apartment. The thread included photos, videos, and drawings of the child, captivating millions of readers. While many believe it was a fictional story, the eerie details made it a viral sensation.

QUIZ

205. True or False: The famous line from the *Jaws* movie, "You're gonna need a bigger boat," was improvised by Roy Scheider.

206. What Japanese urban legend involves a ghostly woman with a slit mouth who asks, "Am I beautiful?"

    A. Teke Teke
    B. Kuchisake-onna
    C. Okiku's Ghost
    D. Yurei Bride

207. True or False: The Aokigahara Forest at the base of Mount Fuji is also known as the "Sea of Trees" and is infamous for its association with suicides.

208. The legend of the cursed _____ Sword involves a blade believed to bring death or misfortune to its owner.

209. The urban legend of _____ Station tells of a mysterious train station that leads passengers to another world or their deaths.

210. What is the title of John Durgin's debut horror novel, which blends small-town horror with supernatural elements?

    A. Consumed by Evil
    B. The Cursed Among Us
    C. Blood Harvest
    D. The Hollowing

ANSWERS

205. *True*

The line, "You're gonna need a bigger boat," delivered by Roy Scheider as Chief Brody, was not in the original script. It was improvised on set and became one of the most quoted lines in movie history, perfectly capturing the terror of encountering the shark.

206. *B. Kuchisake-onna*

Kuchisake-onna, or the "Slit-Mouthed Woman," is a terrifying urban legend. Said to wear a surgical mask, she approaches victims and asks if they find her beautiful. If they say no, she kills them; if they say yes, she reveals her grotesque face and attacks them anyway. The story reflects Japan's love of chilling ghost tales.

207. *True*

Aokigahara Forest, known as the "Sea of Trees," is both a natural wonder and a place of sorrow. The forest's dense foliage and eerie silence have made it a site for those seeking solitude, often tragically leading to suicide. Despite its beauty, it's shrouded in legends of spirits and ghostly encounters.

208. *Muramasa*

The Muramasa Sword, crafted by the legendary swordsmith Muramasa Sengo, is rumored to be cursed. Stories claim it drives its wielder to madness and violence, leading to death and destruction. The legend of the cursed blade has inspired countless tales of haunted artifacts in Japanese folklore.

209. *Kisaragi*

The Kisaragi Station legend began as a creepypasta on a Japanese message board. A user claimed to be stranded at a mysterious station that didn't appear on any map. As the story unfolded in real time, it ended with the user vanishing, leaving readers to wonder if it was a fictional tale or something more sinister.

210. *B. The Cursed Among Us*

John Durgin's debut novel *The Cursed Among Us* introduces readers to a chilling tale of small-town horror, nostalgia, and supernatural terror. Durgin is known for his ability to craft deeply atmospheric settings and relatable characters, making him a rising star in modern horror fiction.

QUIZ

211. What Japanese yokai is said to haunt public restrooms, asking visitors if they want red or blue paper?

   A. Aka Manto
   B. Hanako-san
   C. Noppera-bo
   D. Yuki-onna

212. Which 2007 movie was inspired by the true story of the Zodiac Killer?

   A. Gone Girl
   B. Se7en
   C. Zodiac
   D. The Girl with the Dragon Tattoo

213. True or False: The Yurei ghost is often depicted in white funeral clothing and long, unkempt hair.

214. Which horror author reportedly wrote one of their most famous novels during a drug binge and later claimed not to remember writing it?

   A. Stephen King
   B. H.P. Lovecraft
   C. Clive Barker
   D. Shirley Jackson

215. True or False: Edgar Allan Poe married his 13-year-old cousin, Virginia Clemm.

216. H.P. Lovecraft's infamous monster Cthulhu first appeared in his short story "The Call of _____."

ANSWERS

211. A. Aka Manto

Aka Manto, or the "Red Cloak," is a yokai that haunts bathrooms, offering visitors red or blue paper. Choosing red results in a gruesome death, while blue means strangulation. The only way to escape is to refuse both options. This eerie legend continues to terrify schoolchildren across Japan.

212. C. Zodiac

David Fincher's *Zodiac* meticulously chronicles the investigation into the Zodiac Killer, who terrorized California in the late 1960s and early 1970s. The film, based on Robert Graysmith's books, delves into the taunting letters, ciphers, and the chilling mystery surrounding the killer's identity, which remains unsolved.

213. True

Yurei are vengeful spirits in Japanese folklore, often depicted in white burial clothing with long, disheveled hair. These ghosts, bound to the physical world by unresolved emotions or tragic deaths, appear in classic ghost stories like *Yotsuya Kaidan* and modern films such as *The Grudge* and *The Ring*.

214. A. Stephen King

Stephen King wrote *Cujo* during a period of heavy drug and alcohol abuse. He later admitted that he had no memory of writing the novel, despite its critical acclaim and enduring popularity. King's struggles with addiction during the early part of his career shaped many of his most harrowing works.

215. True

Poe married Virginia Clemm in 1836 when she was just 13 years old, and he was 27. The marriage, while controversial, is often described as a deeply affectionate and supportive relationship. Virginia's early death from tuberculosis profoundly influenced Poe's writing, inspiring themes of loss and despair in his work.

216. Cthulhu

H.P. Lovecraft's *The Call of Cthulhu* introduced readers to the titular cosmic entity in 1928. What's fascinating is that Lovecraft claimed his ideas for the story came to him in dreams. The strange and incomprehensible nature of his creations reflects his fear of the unknown and the insignificance of humanity in the universe.

QUIZ

217. Crystal Lake Publishing's magazine is called Memento Mori Ink. Memento Mori is an artistic or symbolic trope acting as a reminder of _____.

218. What horror author famously feuded with Stanley Kubrick over the adaptation of their novel?

   A. Anne Rice
   B. Stephen King
   C. Shirley Jackson
   D. Richard Matheson

219. True or False: Mary Shelley was just 18 years old when she wrote *Frankenstein*.

220. Anne Rice's most famous novel, *Interview with the Vampire*, was inspired by the death of her young _____.

221. What 1982 sci-fi horror movie by John Carpenter was a remake of a 1951 film?

   A. The Thing
   B. They Live
   C. The Blob
   D. Scanners

222. True or False: Some explorers have claimed to hear strange chanting sounds at night while camping near Machu Picchu.

ANSWERS

217. The inevitability of death

Memento mori literally means "Remember you must die." The early Puritan settlers were particularly aware of death and fearful of what it might mean, so a Puritan tombstone will often display a memento mori intended for the living.

218. B. Stephen King

Stephen King was highly critical of Stanley Kubrick's adaptation of *The Shining*, claiming it strayed too far from the source material. King disliked the portrayal of Jack Torrance and the changes to the Overlook Hotel's atmosphere. Despite King's objections, the film became a horror classic, sparking debates among fans and critics.

219. True

Mary Shelley began writing *Frankenstein* in 1816, during a summer spent at Lord Byron's villa, where the group held a ghost story competition. At only 18 years old, Shelley crafted one of the most influential works of science fiction and horror, solidifying her place as a literary pioneer.

220. Daughter

Anne Rice wrote *Interview with the Vampire* after the death of her five-year-old daughter from leukemia. The themes of loss, immortality, and existential questioning in the novel reflect her grief and struggles. It became the foundation of her iconic *Vampire Chronicles* series.

221. A. The Thing

John Carpenter's *The Thing* is a remake of *The Thing from Another World* (1951) and follows a group of scientists in Antarctica battling a shape-shifting alien. Known for its groundbreaking practical effects, the film initially underperformed but is now regarded as a masterpiece.

222. True

Hikers and researchers camping near Machu Picchu have reported hearing ghostly chanting, drumbeats, and whispers at night. These sounds are often attributed to the spirits of those who died during its construction or were sacrificed to the gods.

QUIZ

223. True or False: Kevin Bacon survived to the end in the original *Friday the 13th*.

224. True or False: A Facebook Marketplace listing for an antique mirror went viral after the seller claimed it was cursed and caused shadows to appear in their home.

225. What horror author allegedly carried around a vial of their own blood for promotional purposes?

   A. Clive Barker
   B. Anne Rice
   C. Poppy Z. Brite
   D. Stephen King

226. True or False: Shirley Jackson's short story *The Lottery* was so controversial that it caused readers to cancel their subscriptions to *The New Yorker*.

227. Which horror author lived in a house they believed was haunted and wrote about it in their work?

   A. Shirley Jackson
   B. Anne Rice
   C. Richard Matheson
   D. Peter Straub

228. True or False: H.P. Lovecraft wrote letters to Harry Houdini and even ghostwrote a story for him.

223. False

Bacon's character, Jack, meets one of the franchise's most iconic deaths—arrow through the neck from beneath the bed. Classic slasher surprise.

224. True

The seller warned buyers that the mirror caused strange shadows and whispering sounds, insisting it be purchased "at your own risk." The listing gained traction in paranormal groups, with many users speculating about its history and others eager to buy it for their collection.

225. C. Poppy Z. Brite

Poppy Z. Brite, known for their dark and visceral horror novels, once used a vial of their own blood as part of a promotional stunt. This macabre act added to their reputation for pushing boundaries in both fiction and life, aligning with the provocative nature of their work.

226. True

When *The Lottery* was published in *The New Yorker* in 1948, it shocked readers with its depiction of small-town ritualistic violence. Many were so disturbed by the story that they canceled their subscriptions, while others sent hate mail to Jackson. The story's critique of conformity and mob mentality has since made it a classic.

227. A. Shirley Jackson

Shirley Jackson drew inspiration for her chilling stories from her belief that her home in North Bennington, Vermont, was haunted. This influence is particularly evident in *The Haunting of Hill House*, considered one of the best ghost stories ever written. Her ability to blend the supernatural with psychological horror has made her work timeless.

228. True

Lovecraft collaborated with Harry Houdini, ghostwriting the story *Under the Pyramids* (also known as *Imprisoned with the Pharaohs*). The tale, based on an idea by Houdini, involves Egyptian mysteries and Lovecraft's signature cosmic horror. Their correspondence highlights Lovecraft's fascination with the supernatural and Houdini's interest in debunking it.

229. Bram Stoker's *Dracula* was partly inspired by a real-life _____ epidemic in the 19th century.

230. What was the title of Graham Masterton's debut horror novel, which became a classic of the genre?

    A. The Manitou
    B. Charnel House
    C. Ritual
    D. The Djinn

231. True or False: The hashtag #HauntedTikTok has amassed over 10 billion views, featuring everything from ghostly encounters to cursed objects.

232. What horror author famously said, "To write something, you have to risk making a fool of yourself"?

    A. Stephen King
    B. Ray Bradbury
    C. Clive Barker
    D. Dean Koontz

233. A TikTok user claimed to document time travel after posting videos of an eerily empty city, dubbing themselves the "Last Man in _____."

234. True or False: Anne Rice once planned to write a novel about werewolves but abandoned the idea after her research scared her too much.

ANSWERS

229. Rabies

Bram Stoker drew inspiration for *Dracula* from contemporary accounts of rabies outbreaks. The disease's symptoms—hypersensitivity, aggression, and fear of water—parallel vampire lore. Stoker blended these elements with folklore about blood-drinking monsters, creating one of the most iconic characters in horror.

230. A. The Manitou

Graham Masterton's debut horror novel, *The Manitou* (1976), introduced readers to a terrifying tale of a Native American shaman reincarnated in modern times. The book's success established Masterton as a leading voice in horror fiction and inspired a cult classic film adaptation in 1978. Known for blending folklore, mythology, and visceral horror, Masterton's prolific career spans novels, short stories, and even influential works on writing and self-help.

231. True

#HauntedTikTok includes a vast collection of videos showcasing supposed paranormal activity. From ghostly figures caught on camera to cursed dolls and Ouija board sessions gone wrong, the hashtag has become a hub for both skeptics and believers to share and debate spooky experiences.

232. B. Ray Bradbury

Ray Bradbury, best known for *Something Wicked This Way Comes* and *The October Country*, often explored the dark side of human nature. His advice to writers emphasized creativity and bravery, encouraging them to embrace vulnerability. Bradbury's mix of horror, science fiction, and fantasy cemented his legacy as a literary innovator.

233. Spain

A user named @unicosobreviviente (translated as "The Last Survivor") gained attention for videos claiming to document a future where they are the only person alive in Spain. The empty streets, malls, and public spaces sparked theories of time travel, alternate dimensions, and CGI trickery.

234. False

While Anne Rice didn't abandon the idea, she did write a werewolf novel, *The Wolf Gift*. Her meticulous research and ability to humanize monsters are evident in all her works. Rice's exploration of werewolves added another layer to her supernatural universe, alongside her iconic vampires.

235. Richard Matheson's *I Am Legend* is often credited with inspiring the modern _____ genre.

236. What horror author worked as an undertaker before achieving literary success?

   A. R.L. Stine
   B. Clive Barker
   C. Brian Lumley
   D. Thomas Ligotti

237. True or False: Edgar Allan Poe was expelled from West Point for showing up to a military drill naked.

238. Which U.S. president wrote a story about a haunted house?

   A. Abraham Lincoln
   B. Thomas Jefferson
   C. Jimmy Carter
   D. Ronald Reagan

239. True or False: Mark Twain, best known for his humorous and satirical works, also wrote a ghost story.

240. *The Legend of Sleepy Hollow* author Washington Irving also wrote a spooky tale called "The Adventure of the _____ Student."

ANSWERS

235. *Zombie*

While *I Am Legend* focuses on vampires, its depiction of a lone survivor battling infected creatures influenced the modern zombie genre. George Romero cited Matheson's novel as an inspiration for *Night of the Living Dead*, bridging the gap between vampires and zombies in popular culture.

236. *C. Brian Lumley*

Brian Lumley, author of the *Necroscope* series, worked as an undertaker early in his career. His experiences with death and the macabre greatly influenced his writing, blending supernatural horror with a keen understanding of mortality.

237. *True*

Edgar Allan Poe was expelled from the United States Military Academy at West Point in 1831. According to some accounts, he deliberately committed infractions to provoke his dismissal, including attending drills wearing only his belt and gloves. His rebellious nature carried into his work, where he defied conventions and delved into the macabre.

238. *A. Abraham Lincoln*

Abraham Lincoln wrote a short story called *The Trailor Murder Mystery*, which involves a mysterious murder and an eerie house. While not explicitly horror, it showcases Lincoln's creative side and his interest in storytelling. This lesser-known fact adds a spooky twist to his legacy as a president.

239. *True*

Mark Twain wrote *A Ghost Story*, a humorous yet eerie tale about a man spending the night in a haunted room. The ghost turns out to be the Cardiff Giant, a famous hoax from Twain's time. Twain's wit shines even in his foray into supernatural fiction, blending comedy with chills.

240. *German*

Washington Irving's *The Adventure of the German Student* is a dark tale involving a mysterious woman and a spectral twist. Best known for *The Legend of Sleepy Hollow* and *Rip Van Winkle*, Irving's Gothic tales contributed to the foundation of American horror literature.

241. What famous actor co-wrote a horror novel titled *Gump and Co.*?

    A. Tom Hanks
    B. Michael Caine
    C. Gene Hackman
    D. Burt Reynolds

242. True or False: Stephen King once collaborated with Bruce Springsteen on a short horror story.

243. Horror legend Vincent Price co-wrote a book titled *A Treasury of Great* _____.

244. Which tagline is famously associated with the movie *Alien*?

    A. "In space, no one can hear you scream."
    B. "They're here."
    C. "Be afraid. Be very afraid."
    D. "Who will survive and what will be left of them?"

245. What celebrity author wrote *The Burial*, a vampire novel, in the 1990s?

    A. Michael Jackson
    B. Marilyn Manson
    C. Christopher Lee
    D. Nick Cave

246. Which Andrew van Wey novel explores a cursed painting that leads to psychological and supernatural horrors?

    A. The Unveiled
    B. Forsaken
    C. The Grim Light
    D. The Rorschach Canvas

ANSWERS

241. C. Gene Hackman

Gene Hackman co-wrote *Wake of the Perdido Star*, a historical adventure novel with dark and eerie undertones. While not strictly horror, the book showcases Hackman's talent for creating suspense and intrigue, surprising fans of his acting career.

242. False

While Stephen King and Bruce Springsteen share a love of dark storytelling, they have never collaborated. However, King has worked with other musicians, such as John Mellencamp, on projects blending music and horror.

243. Recipes

Vincent Price, known for his iconic roles in horror films, co-wrote *A Treasury of Great Recipes* with his wife, Mary. The book showcases their love of cooking, with some dishes carrying macabre themes, blending Price's culinary passion with his horror legacy.

244. A. "In space, no one can hear you scream."

Directed by Ridley Scott, *Alien* combines science fiction and horror as the crew of the spaceship Nostromo encounters a deadly extraterrestrial creature. The chilling tagline emphasizes the isolation and terror of space.

245. D. Nick Cave

Musician and writer Nick Cave penned *And the Ass Saw the Angel* and *The Death of Bunny Munro*, exploring dark and twisted themes. *The Burial* is a lesser-known work showcasing his flair for blending horror with existential dread, reflecting his gothic persona.

246. D. The Rorschach Canvas

Andrew van Wey's *The Rorschach Canvas* delves into the eerie tale of a cursed painting that drives its owners to madness and despair. Known for his atmospheric prose and ability to blur the lines between reality and the supernatural, van Wey's work is a must-read for fans of psychological horror.

QUIZ

247. True or False: The poet Edgar Allan Poe was once rumored to have worked on a story with Charles Dickens.

248. What infamous house in New York became the setting for *The Amityville Horror*?

    A. 112 Ocean Avenue
    B. 221B Baker Street
    C. The Winchester House
    D. The Perron Farm

249. True or False: The Winchester Mystery House was built by Sarah Winchester to confuse the spirits of those killed by Winchester rifles.

250. Which 1999 supernatural thriller, based on a Richard Matheson novel, starred Kevin Bacon?

    A. The Sixth Sense
    B. Stir of Echoes
    C. The Haunting
    D. What Lies Beneath

251. The _____ Plantation in Louisiana is rumored to be haunted by the ghosts of slaves and a mysterious woman in white.

252. What haunted house in San Diego is famous for its violent ghostly encounters and once housed a family that fled in terror?

    A. The Villisca Axe Murder House
    B. The Whaley House
    C. The LaLaurie Mansion
    D. The Riddle House

ANSWERS

247. *True*

While they never officially collaborated, Edgar Allan Poe and Charles Dickens admired each other's work and corresponded briefly. Poe even reviewed Dickens's works, and their mutual fascination with the macabre often led to speculation about a potential collaboration.

248. *A. 112 Ocean Avenue*

The house at 112 Ocean Avenue in Amityville, New York, gained notoriety after the Lutz family claimed they experienced paranormal activity following the murder of six family members by Ronald DeFeo Jr. in 1974. Their story inspired a bestselling book and a film franchise, though skeptics debate the veracity of the claims.

249. *True*

Sarah Winchester, heiress to the Winchester rifle fortune, continuously expanded her San Jose mansion for 38 years, creating a labyrinth of staircases to nowhere and doors that open into walls. She believed the construction would appease or confuse the spirits of those killed by her family's rifles.

250. *B. Stir of Echoes*

Matheson's novel *A Stir of Echoes* was adapted into the 1999 film *Stir of Echoes*, starring Kevin Bacon. The story follows a man who gains psychic abilities after being hypnotized, leading to disturbing visions and a murder mystery. Matheson's knack for blending the supernatural with human drama is on full display in this tale.

251. *Myrtles*

The Myrtles Plantation, built in 1796, is one of America's most haunted homes. Tales of ghostly children, a haunted mirror, and the spirit of Chloe, a former enslaved woman, have made it a hotspot for paranormal investigators and thrill-seekers.

252. *B. The Whaley House*

The Whaley House in San Diego, built in 1857, is considered one of the most haunted houses in America. The property's history includes executions, suicides, and mysterious deaths. Visitors report hearing disembodied voices, seeing ghostly figures, and feeling an overwhelming sense of dread.

253. True or False: The LaLaurie Mansion in New Orleans was once owned by a notorious socialite known for torturing enslaved people.

254. The Borley _____, often called "the most haunted house in England," was reportedly the site of ghostly nuns, footsteps, and mysterious writings on walls.

255. What haunted house in Kansas is known for paranormal investigations and a past involving gruesome murders?

   A. The Sallie House
   B. The Lizzie Borden House
   C. The H.H. Holmes Murder Castle
   D. The Riddle House

256. True or False: The Lizzie Borden House in Massachusetts operates as a bed-and breakfast where guests can sleep in the room where her stepmother was murdered.

257. What serial killer claimed to have murdered 93 people and is considered one of the most prolific in U.S. history?

   A. Ted Bundy
   B. John Wayne Gacy
   C. Samuel Little
   D. Jeffrey Dahmer

258. Crystal Lake Publishing was founded in _____ South Africa, in the same city where author J.R.R. Tolkien was born.

253. True

The LaLaurie Mansion in New Orleans was the home of Madame Delphine LaLaurie, a wealthy socialite whose horrific abuse of enslaved people was uncovered in the 1830s. The house is said to be haunted by the spirits of her victims, and its gruesome history has inspired countless ghost stories and films.

254. Rectory

The Borley Rectory in Essex, England, gained fame in the early 20th century for its intense paranormal activity. Reports included sightings of ghostly figures, strange noises, and poltergeist activity. While some accounts were debunked, the rectory's reputation as a paranormal hotspot persists.

255. A. The Sallie House

The Sallie House in Atchison, Kansas, is named after a young girl whose ghost is said to haunt the home. Paranormal investigators have reported scratches, objects moving on their own, and mysterious voices. The house's dark history has made it a staple of ghost-hunting lore.

256. True

The Lizzie Borden House, where Andrew and Abby Borden were infamously murdered with an axe in 1892, is now a bed-and-breakfast. Visitors can stay in the crime scene rooms and participate in ghost tours, adding a macabre twist to the historic home's legacy.

257. C. Samuel Little

Samuel Little confessed to killing 93 people, mostly women, between 1970 and 2005. The FBI has confirmed over 60 of his confessions, making him one of the most prolific serial killers in U.S. history. Little's detailed drawings of his victims helped identify previously unsolved cases.

258. Bloemfontein

Crystal Lake's founder and CEO, Joe Mynhardt, founded by Crystal Lake while teaching primary school. John Ronald Reuel Tolkien, author of *The Hobbit* and *The Lord of the Rings*, was born in Bloemfontein, an Afrikaans-speaking area of South Africa, on 3 January 1892. His father had become a bank manager there.

QUIZ

259. True or False: Ed Gein, the real-life inspiration for Leatherface, Buffalo Bill, and Norman Bates, made furniture and clothing out of human skin.

260. The Zodiac Killer's identity remains a mystery, but he taunted police with cryptic _____ sent to newspapers.

261. What serial killer worked as a clown at children's parties, earning him the nickname "The Killer Clown"?

    A. Jeffrey Dahmer
    B. Ted Bundy
    C. John Wayne Gacy
    D. Richard Ramirez

262. True or False: Jack the Ripper, London's infamous serial killer, was never identified.

263. What groundbreaking decision did Alfred Hitchcock make regarding audience entry during *Psycho* screenings?

    A. Audience members couldn't leave once the film started.
    B. No one was allowed into the theater after the movie began.
    C. Viewers had to sign a waiver acknowledging the film's intensity.
    D. The film played without an intermission to maintain tension.

264. The "Night Stalker," Richard Ramirez, broke into homes in California during the 1980s, leaving behind satanic _____.

ANSWERS

259. True

Ed Gein, a murderer and grave robber from Wisconsin, was infamous for exhuming corpses and creating macabre items like lampshades, belts, and masks from human skin. His grotesque crimes inspired some of the most iconic characters in horror, solidifying his dark legacy.

260. Ciphers

The Zodiac Killer terrorized California in the late 1960s, claiming responsibility for multiple murders. He sent letters and ciphers to newspapers, some of which remain unsolved. Despite numerous suspects and theories, his identity has never been confirmed, keeping his case one of the most chilling mysteries in criminal history.

261. C. John Wayne Gacy

John Wayne Gacy was a respected community member in Illinois who performed as "Pogo the Clown" at events. Beneath this facade, he was a sadistic killer responsible for the deaths of at least 33 young men and boys. His dual life and gruesome crimes have cemented his place in infamy.

262. False

Jack the Ripper terrorized London's Whitechapel district in 1888, killing and mutilating at least five women. This murderer was identified in 2025 as Aaron Kosminski, a Polish barber who was a suspect at the time of the murders. His gruesome methods and taunting letters to the police have made him one of history's most infamous killers.

263. B. No one was allowed into the theater after the movie began.

Hitchcock insisted that no one be admitted after the film started to preserve the story's surprises, particularly the shocking mid-film death of Marion Crane. This rule revolutionized how audiences experienced suspense in cinema.

264. Symbols

Richard Ramirez, known as the "Night Stalker," was a brutal serial killer who targeted homes across California. He left pentagrams and other satanic symbols at crime scenes, claiming to act on behalf of Satan. Ramirez's chilling methods and lack of remorse made him a terrifying figure during his reign of terror.

QUIZ

265. What is the name of the very first board game publishing by the South African small press, Crystal Lake Publishing (yes, they published this book):

   A. Night of the Living Dead
   B. Mean Spirited
   C. Ghostland
   D. The Newport Curse

266. What infamous killer was known for his chilling ability to charm victims and even escaped custody twice?

   A. Jeffrey Dahmer
   B. Ted Bundy
   C. Aileen Wuornos
   D. Albert Fish

267. True or False: Albert Fish, known as "The Gray Man," claimed to have killed and eaten children.

268. Which "scary" Halloween costume is statistically the most common?

   A. Ghost
   B. Vampire
   C. Witch
   D. Sexy Cat

269. True or False: Dracula was originally going to be called "Count Wampyr."

270. The fear of Halloween is called _____.

ANSWERS

265. C. Ghostland

Crystal Lake Publishing's very first venture into the gaming world is a *Ghostland* board game based on Duncan Ralston's novel. The game will bring the terrifying amusement park concept from the book to life, allowing players to navigate haunted attractions, encounter ghosts, and survive the horrors that unfold. It's designed to be immersive, strategic, and filled with eerie surprises, capturing the essence of *Ghostland's* supernatural chaos.

266. B. Ted Bundy

Ted Bundy used his charisma and good looks to lure victims, often feigning injury to gain their trust. He escaped custody twice, once jumping from a courthouse window and later tunneling out of jail. His cunning nature and horrific crimes have made him one of the most studied serial killers in history.

267. True

Albert Fish, a deranged killer and cannibal, preyed on children in the early 20th century. He sent a horrifying letter to one victim's family, detailing his crimes. Fish's depravity shocked even seasoned investigators, earning him a place among the most sadistic killers in history.

268. C. Witch

Year after year, the witch remains the most popular Halloween costume. From creepy hags to stylish sorceresses, witches dominate the spooky season, proving that pointy hats and broomsticks never go out of style.

269. True

Bram Stoker's original notes reveal that his famous vampire was initially named Count Wampyr before he stumbled upon the name "Dracula." Count Wampyr doesn't quite have the same bite.

270. Samhainophobia

Samhainophobia, the fear of Halloween, might seem ironic to those who enjoy costumes and candy. But for some, the spooky decorations and creepy vibes are just too much to handle.

QUIZ

271. Which Jasper Bark novel is known for blending extreme horror with dark humor, earning a reputation as a modern cult classic?

    A. Quiet Places
    B. Stuck on You
    C. Way of the Barefoot Zombie
    D. The Final Cut

272. What haunted house attraction holds the record for the most lawsuits from terrified guests?

    A. The 13th Gate
    B. McKamey Manor
    C. The Haunted Mansion
    D. Spooky World

273. True or False: The "Bloody Mary" urban legend has caused mirror sales to drop significantly during Halloween.

274. Zombies are often depicted shambling, but in 2002's *28 Days Later*, they were terrifyingly _____.

275. What spooky creature has its own annual festival in Point Pleasant, West Virginia?

    A. The Jersey Devil
    B. Bigfoot
    C. The Mothman
    D. Dracula

276. True or False: The original Frankenstein movie (1931) was banned in some places for being too scary.

277. What legendary serial killer was nicknamed "The Acid Bath Murderer" due to his gruesome method of disposing of bodies?

    A. Albert Fish
    B. John George Haigh
    C. Peter Sutcliffe
    D. Harold Shipman

ANSWERS

271. B. Stuck on You

Jasper Bark's *Stuck on You* is a visceral and shocking tale that combines extreme horror with his signature dark humor. Known for pushing boundaries and delivering unforgettable stories, Bark has become a favorite among fans of transgressive and unconventional horror fiction.

272. B. McKamey Manor

McKamey Manor is infamous for being less of a haunted house and more of a psychological endurance test. Guests are required to sign a 40-page waiver, and no one has ever made it to the end.

273. False

While Bloody Mary is a chilling legend, she's not breaking any mirrors—just scaring people into cleaning theirs before attempting the ritual.

274. Fast

The zombies in *28 Days Later* don't shuffle; they sprint like they've just had an espresso shot. This change revolutionized zombie movies and made everyone rethink their cardio game in case of an outbreak.

275. C. The Mothman

The Mothman Festival celebrates this winged cryptid with costumes, pancakes, and plenty of conspiracy theories. Where else can you see a parade of Mothman impersonators AND learn about local UFO sightings?

276. True

Audiences in the 1930s found *Frankenstein* so frightening that some theaters refused to screen it.

277. B. John George Haigh

John George Haigh, active in the 1940s, used acid to dissolve the bodies of his victims, believing this would destroy all evidence of his crimes. However, investigators uncovered enough remains to convict him, cementing his macabre nickname.

278. True or False: The Black Monk of Pontefract is considered one of the most violent poltergeists in history.

279. What is the name of the British Fantasy Award's most prestigious honor for a novel?

    A. The August Derleth Award
    B. The Arthur Machen Prize
    C. The Mary Shelley Award
    D. The Robert Aickman Medal

280. The Donner Party's ill-fated expedition involved pioneers resorting to _____ to survive.

281. Which 19th-century killer operated in Chicago, building a "Murder Castle" filled with trap doors and secret passageways?

    A. Albert Fish
    B. H.H. Holmes
    C. Belle Gunness
    D. Jack the Ripper

282. True or False: The Salem Witch Trials led to the execution of both men and women.

283. The Axeman of _____ sent letters to newspapers, promising not to kill anyone who played jazz in their homes.

ANSWERS

278. True

The Black Monk of Pontefract allegedly haunted a house in Yorkshire, England, during the 1960s. Known for throwing objects, slamming doors, and terrifying the Pritchard family, the entity is rumored to be the spirit of a 16th-century monk executed for murder.

279. A. The August Derleth Award

The British Fantasy Award's August Derleth Award is presented annually for the best horror or dark fantasy novel. Named after the influential writer and publisher who helped popularize H.P. Lovecraft's works, this accolade is a cornerstone of the British Fantasy Society's celebration of speculative fiction.

280. Cannibalism

Trapped by heavy snow in the Sierra Nevada in 1846, the Donner Party resorted to cannibalism to survive. The harrowing story of desperation and survival is one of the darkest chapters in American pioneer history.

281. B. H.H. Holmes

H.H. Holmes constructed a labyrinthine building during the 1893 Chicago World's Fair, complete with soundproof rooms and deadly traps. Dubbed the "Murder Castle," it became a nightmare for his unsuspecting victims and a chilling monument to his cruelty.

282. True

While women were the primary targets of the Salem Witch Trials, men were also accused and executed. Giles Corey, for example, was pressed to death under heavy stones for refusing to enter a plea. The trials remain a dark testament to mass hysteria and injustice.

283. New Orleans

Active in the early 20th century, the Axeman of New Orleans was a serial killer who claimed to love jazz. In one infamous letter, he declared he would spare homes playing jazz music on a specific night, turning the city into an eerie, music-filled frenzy.

284. Which author is celebrated for their Southern Gothic horror debut, *The Between*?

    A. Tananarive Due
    B. Cherie Priest
    C. Hailey Piper
    D. Ania Ahlborn

285. Who plays the young Norman Bates in the TV series *Bates Motel* (2013–2017)?

    A. Asa Butterfield
    B. Evan Peters
    C. Freddie Highmore
    D. Logan Lerman

286. True or False: The Bell Witch haunting in Tennessee involved a spirit that physically attacked a family.

287. What unsolved 1996 murder case involved the death of a six-year-old beauty pageant contestant in her family's home?

    A. JonBenét Ramsey
    B. Caylee Anthony
    C. Amber Hagerman
    D. Polly Klaas

288. True or False: The Dyatlov Pass incident was officially declared solved in 2020.

289. The disappearance of Malaysia Airlines Flight _____ in 2014 remains one of the greatest aviation mysteries of all time.

ANSWERS

284. A. Tananarive Due

Tananarive Due's *The Between* explores themes of race, identity, and the supernatural through a Southern Gothic lens. A pioneer of modern horror, Due has influenced a new generation of writers while continuing to craft haunting and thought-provoking stories.

285. C. Freddie Highmore

Freddie Highmore gave a chilling and nuanced performance as teenage Norman Bates in this *Psycho* prequel, slowly unraveling into the infamous killer we know from Hitchcock's classic. His chemistry with Vera Farmiga (Norma Bates) carried the entire series.

286. True

The Bell Witch haunting, which occurred in the early 1800s, involved a malicious spirit tormenting the Bell family. Reports include physical attacks, eerie voices, and mysterious phenomena. The haunting became so infamous that even Andrew Jackson is said to have visited the site.

287. A. JonBenét Ramsey

JonBenét Ramsey's murder remains one of the most infamous cold cases in modern history. Found in her family's basement in Boulder, Colorado, the case has been plagued by mishandled evidence and countless theories, leaving her tragic death shrouded in mystery.

288. False

While a 2020 investigation suggested an avalanche as the cause of the 1959 Dyatlov Pass incident, skeptics argue that the mysterious injuries, radiation, and missing body parts don't align with this explanation. The case continues to haunt investigators and enthusiasts alike.

289. MH370

Malaysia Airlines Flight MH370 vanished en route to Beijing, sparking one of the largest search efforts in aviation history. Despite debris being found years later, the exact cause of the disappearance and the fate of its 239 passengers and crew remain unknown.

QUIZ

290. What 2017 Netflix documentary brought worldwide attention to the strange case of Elisa Lam's death in a Los Angeles hotel?

   A. Making a Murderer
   B. The Staircase
   C. Crime Scene: The Vanishing at the Cecil Hotel
   D. Don't F**k with Cats

291. True or False: In 2021, scientists identified a possible cause of Havana Syndrome, a mysterious illness affecting U.S. diplomats.

292. The _____ Forest in Romania is often called the "Bermuda Triangle of Transylvania" duc to its strange disappearances and ghostly phenomena.

293. What 2018 case involved the family annihilation committed by Chris Watts, which shocked the world due to his calm demeanor in media interviews?

   A. The Peterson Case
   B. The Watts Family Murders
   C. The Laci Peterson Case
   D. The McStay Family Case

294. What creepy TikTok series involved a man documenting his encounters with a mysterious figure outside his home, eventually leading to claims he went missing?

   A. The Smiling Man
   B. Dear David
   C. Final Transmission
   D. Him in the Shadows

295. True or False: The 2019 Notre Dame fire was immediately ruled accidental, with no suspicion of arson.

ANSWERS

290. C. Crime Scene: The Vanishing at the Cecil Hotel

Elisa Lam's body was found in the water tank of the Cecil Hotel after strange footage of her acting erratically in an elevator went viral. While her death was ruled accidental, the bizarre circumstances and the hotel's dark history sparked theories of foul play and supernatural involvement.

291. True

Havana Syndrome, first reported in 2016, involves symptoms like dizziness, headaches, and hearing strange noises. In 2021, experts suggested directed energy attacks as a possible cause, though the phenomenon remains largely unexplained, fueling conspiracy theories about espionage and advanced weaponry.

292. Hoia-Baciu

The Hoia-Baciu Forest is infamous for UFO sightings, disembodied voices, and unexplained disappearances. Its eerie, twisted trees and unsettling atmosphere have made it a hotspot for paranormal investigators and thrill-seekers alike.

293. B. The Watts Family Murders

Chris Watts confessed to murdering his pregnant wife and two young daughters in 2018. The chilling details, combined with his calm media appearances, horrified the public. The case gained renewed attention through documentaries and continues to serve as a cautionary tale about hidden darkness.

294. A. The Smiling Man

The *Smiling Man* series featured a TikTok user sharing videos of a shadowy figure standing outside his house, smiling ominously. The series ended abruptly, with the creator claiming the figure had taken him. While many believe it was an elaborate story, its chilling realism captivated viewers.

295. True

The Notre Dame Cathedral fire devastated the iconic structure in April 2019. Investigations concluded it was likely caused by an electrical short or a cigarette, though conspiracy theories initially swirled. The rebuilding effort continues to this day, blending sorrow with hope.

296. What was the name of the Canadian killer whose disturbing videos led to an international manhunt chronicled in *Don't F**k with Cats*?

    A. Paul Bernardo
    B. Luka Magnotta
    C. Karla Homolka
    D. Mark Twitchell

297. What American man spent 9 years on death row for a crime he didn't commit before being exonerated by DNA evidence?

    A. Steven Avery
    B. Anthony Ray Hinton
    C. Damien Echols
    D. Kirk Bloodsworth

298. The ancient Egyptian Book of the Dead was a guide to navigating the _____.

299. True or False: The Central Park Five were teenagers wrongly convicted of a brutal assault in New York's Central Park in 1989.

300. The West Memphis _____ were three teenagers wrongfully convicted of murder in Arkansas, largely based on circumstantial evidence and accusations of satanic ritual involvement.

301. What chilling case involved a man wrongly convicted of his wife's murder after she was found at the bottom of a staircase?

    A. Michael Peterson
    B. Scott Peterson
    C. Todd Willingham
    D. Larry Swearingen

ANSWERS

296. B. Luka Magnotta

Luka Magnotta gained notoriety after posting horrifying videos of animal cruelty online, which led internet sleuths to uncover his identity. The hunt took a darker turn when Magnotta murdered Jun Lin, a Chinese student, and mailed body parts to Canadian political offices. The documentary showcases the chilling power of online communities in solving crimes while exploring the dangerous obsession of true crime fanatics.

297. D. Kirk Bloodsworth

Kirk Bloodsworth was wrongfully convicted of the rape and murder of a young girl in 1984. In 1993, DNA evidence proved his innocence, making him the first U.S. death row inmate exonerated by DNA testing. His story highlights the devastating consequences of wrongful convictions.

298. Afterlife

The Book of the Dead was a collection of spells, prayers, and rituals designed to help the deceased navigate the dangers of the afterlife and reach the Field of Reeds, a paradise in Egyptian mythology. These texts were often inscribed on papyrus and placed in tombs to protect the soul.

299. True

The Central Park Five—Kevin Richardson, Raymond Santana, Antron McCray, Yusef Salaam, and Korey Wise—were coerced into confessing to the assault and rape of a jogger. They spent years in prison before DNA evidence and a confession from the real perpetrator cleared their names. Their case became a symbol of systemic injustice.

300. Three

Damien Echols, Jason Baldwin, and Jessie Misskelley were convicted of killing three young boys in 1993. The trial was marked by public hysteria over alleged satanic rituals. After years of advocacy and new evidence, they were released in 2011, though they were forced to take an Alford plea, maintaining their innocence.

301. A. Michael Peterson

Michael Peterson's case became infamous after the documentary *The Staircase*. Convicted of murdering his wife, Kathleen, in 2001, Peterson's trial revealed questionable forensic practices. He was eventually granted a new trial and released in 2017 after entering an Alford plea, maintaining his innocence.

302. True or False: Rubin "Hurricane" Carter, a professional boxer, was falsely convicted of murder in the 1960s.

303. Which New York Times bestselling author's Joe Ledger series was turned into a graphic novel by Crystal Lake Publishing?

   A. Clive Barker
   B. Richard Chizmar
   C. Jonathan Maberry
   D. Richard Matheson

304. The wrongful conviction of Thomas Haynesworth, who served 27 years for rape, was overturned when DNA evidence revealed the real attacker, nicknamed the _____ Rapist.

305. What chilling case involved a man who was executed after being convicted based on arson evidence later proven scientifically invalid?

   A. Cameron Todd Willingham
   B. Troy Davis
   C. Brandon Mayfield
   D. Carlos DeLuna

306. True or False: The "Guildford Four" spent over 15 years in prison for IRA bombings they did not commit.

307. What 1975 UFO abduction case inspired the movie *Fire in the Sky*?

   A. The Roswell Incident
   B. The Travis Walton Abduction
   C. The Betty and Barney Hill Case
   D. The Allagash Incident

ANSWERS

302. *True*

Rubin Carter was convicted of a triple homicide in 1966, despite shaky evidence and alleged racial bias in the investigation. After nearly 20 years in prison, his conviction was overturned in 1985. His story inspired the Bob Dylan song "Hurricane" and remains a powerful example of wrongful imprisonment.

303. *Jonathan Maberry*

Jonathan Maberry's *Joe Ledger* series, a thrilling blend of action, horror, and sci-fi, follows the adventures of a former detective-turned-elite special ops agent battling bioweapons, genetic monstrosities, and supernatural threats. The series, which began with *Patient Zero*, has been adapted into a graphic novel by Crystal Lake Publishing, bringing its intense, cinematic storytelling to a new visual medium. With its mix of military strategy, bio-horror, and pulse-pounding action, the *Joe Ledger* series has captivated fans of both horror and thriller genres.

304. *Black Widow*

Thomas Haynesworth was arrested in 1984 based on eyewitness misidentification. Decades later, DNA evidence proved his innocence, identifying the true perpetrator as Leon Davis, a serial rapist. Haynesworth's case shed light on the flaws of eyewitness testimony.

305. *A. Cameron Todd Willingham*

Cameron Todd Willingham was executed in Texas in 2004 for allegedly setting a fire that killed his three daughters. Later investigations revealed the forensic evidence used against him was deeply flawed. His case is a haunting reminder of the potential for fatal errors in the justice system.

306. *True*

The Guildford Four were convicted of bombing two pubs in England in 1974. Their convictions were based on coerced confessions and unreliable evidence. In 1989, their convictions were overturned, exposing widespread corruption and misconduct in the investigation.

307. *B. The Travis Walton Abduction*

Travis Walton claimed he was abducted by a UFO while working as a logger in Arizona. Witnesses, including his co-workers, reported seeing a bright light that struck Walton before he disappeared for five days. His sudden return and detailed descriptions of the spacecraft became one of the most famous and controversial UFO abduction cases, later dramatized in the film *Fire in the Sky*.

QUIZ

308. True or False: The Betty and Barney Hill abduction in 1961 is considered the first widely publicized UFO abduction case in the United States.

309. The 1976 Allagash Abductions involved four men who were canoeing in _____.

310. What UFO abduction case involved a man disappearing from his car near Pascagoula, Mississippi, in 1973?

   A. The Cash-Landrum Incident
   B. The Travis Walton Case
   C. The Charles Hickson and Calvin Parker Abduction
   D. The Kelly–Hopkinsville Encounter

311. True or False: Barney Hill's description of the aliens matched later reports of "grey" extraterrestrials.

312. The Rendlesham Forest UFO incident occurred near a U.S. Air Force base in _____, England.

313. What famous paranormal investigation captured alleged ghostly activity on camera at the Borley Rectory, dubbed "the most haunted house in England"?

   A. Harry Price's Investigation
   B. The SPR Experiment
   C. The Enfield Poltergeist Team
   D. The Ghost Club Inquiry

ANSWERS

308. True

Betty and Barney Hill claimed they were abducted by aliens in New Hampshire while driving home from a vacation. They reported undergoing medical examinations aboard a spacecraft. Their case introduced the concept of "missing time" into UFO lore and remains a cornerstone of alien abduction stories.

309. Maine

The Allagash Abductions occurred during a camping trip in Maine when four men claimed to see a bright UFO while canoeing. They later experienced "missing time" and had shared memories of being examined by aliens. Hypnosis sessions revealed strikingly similar accounts, fueling belief in their story.

310. C. The Charles Hickson and Calvin Parker Abduction

Charles Hickson and Calvin Parker claimed they were fishing on the Pascagoula River when a UFO appeared, and they were paralyzed and taken aboard by strange creatures. Their case gained national attention, with Hickson and Parker passing lie detector tests about their experience.

311. True

Barney Hill described the beings as humanoid with large heads and slanted eyes, a description that later became the archetype of "grey" aliens in popular culture. The Hill case helped establish many elements of modern alien abduction stories, from medical examinations to telepathic communication.

312. Suffolk

The Rendlesham Forest incident in December 1980 involved U.S. Air Force personnel witnessing strange lights and a possible UFO landing. Dubbed "Britain's Roswell," it remains one of the most well-documented UFO cases, with official reports, eyewitness accounts, and ongoing debate about what really happened.

313. A. Harry Price's Investigation

Harry Price, a renowned ghost hunter, investigated Borley Rectory in the 1930s. He captured photos of mysterious writing on walls, unexplained lights, and objects moving on their own. While skeptics have debated the validity of his findings, Price's work helped cement Borley Rectory's haunted reputation.

QUIZ

314. True or False: The Enfield Poltergeist case involved police officers who reported witnessing furniture move on its own.

315. The Queen Mary, a retired ocean liner, is infamous for ghostly encounters in its _____.

316. Which famous skeptic reportedly witnessed unexplained activity during a séance, leading to a shift in their beliefs?

    A. Harry Houdini
    B. Arthur Conan Doyle
    C. Michael Faraday
    D. Victor Hugo

317. What South African forest is believed to be haunted, with hikers claiming to hear disembodied voices?

    A. Tsitsikamma Forest
    B. Knysna Forest
    C. Hogsback Forest
    D. Grootvadersbosch

318. Who wrote the novel that Alfred Hitchcock adapted into the film *Psycho*?

    A. Shirley Jackson
    B. Robert Bloch
    C. Richard Matheson
    D. Daphne du Maurier

319. True or False: The Brown Lady of Raynham Hall is one of the most famous ghost photographs ever captured.

ANSWERS

314. True

In the late 1970s, the Enfield Poltergeist terrorized a family in England. Police officers, reporters, and paranormal investigators claimed to witness phenomena, including furniture moving without cause and strange voices emanating from a young girl. The case remains one of the most famous and debated hauntings in modern history.

315. Swimming pool

The Queen Mary, now a floating hotel in California, is famous for ghostly sightings in its swimming pool. Visitors and staff have reported seeing spectral women in 1930s swimsuits and hearing disembodied laughter. The ship's haunted reputation draws thousands of paranormal enthusiasts every year.

316. D. Victor Hugo

Victor Hugo, the famed author of *Les Misérables*, participated in séances while exiled on the Channel Islands. He reportedly witnessed strange phenomena and claimed to have communicated with spirits, including Shakespeare and Jesus. These experiences deeply influenced his views on spirituality and the supernatural.

317. B. Knysna Forest

The Knysna Forest is surrounded by legends of spirits, mysterious disappearances, and ghostly apparitions. Some say the forest is home to the elusive Knysna elephants, while others believe it harbors more supernatural entities. Its dense canopy and eerie silence make it a prime location for chilling tales.

318. B. Robert Bloch

Robert Bloch's 1959 novel *Psycho* served as the basis for Alfred Hitchcock's iconic 1960 film. Bloch's work delves into the twisted mind of Norman Bates, a character inspired by real-life killer Ed Gein. Hitchcock's adaptation closely follows the novel while adding his own masterful cinematic touch, resulting in a classic that redefined the horror genre.

319. True

The Brown Lady of Raynham Hall was photographed in 1936 by Country Life magazine photographers. The image appears to show a ghostly figure descending a staircase and is considered one of the most compelling pieces of paranormal evidence. The photo has never been conclusively debunked, adding to its mystique.

320. The Crescent Hotel in _____, Arkansas, is often called "America's most haunted hotel" due to numerous ghost sightings.

321. What 2007 paranormal investigation captured chilling evidence at a former tuberculosis sanatorium?

   A. The Ghost Adventures Waverly Hills Investigation
   B. The Amityville Horror House Revisit
   C. The Eastern State Penitentiary Experiment
   D. The Myrtles Plantation Night Watch

322. What viral TikTok trend involved people exploring abandoned locations and allegedly discovering paranormal activity?

   A. #HauntedTikTok
   B. #AbandonedPlaces
   C. #Randonautica
   D. #GhostHunters

323. True or False: The movie *Open Water* was inspired by the true story of two divers left behind by their diving group.

324. A viral YouTube series titled *Exploring the* _____ showcases urban explorers venturing into abandoned and haunted locations.

325. What YouTube channel gained notoriety for uploading unsettling videos of a person in a white mask performing cryptic actions?

   A. Marble Hornets
   B. Poppy
   C. This House Has People In It
   D. 0010110

ANSWERS

320. Eureka Springs

The Crescent Hotel in Eureka Springs is infamous for its ghostly activity. Originally built as a luxury hotel, it later became a hospital run by a fraudulent doctor. Guests report encountering spirits of former patients, including a nurse who haunts the hallways and a man who appears in their rooms at night.

321. A. The Ghost Adventures Waverly Hills Investigation

The *Ghost Adventures* team investigated Waverly Hills Sanatorium, capturing chilling evidence, including shadow figures and unexplained voices. Once a tuberculosis hospital, Waverly Hills is notorious for its "death tunnel" and reports of patients' spirits still lingering. The investigation remains a highlight of the paranormal series.

322. C. #Randonautica

The *Randonautica* app sends users to random locations based on their "intentions." Many TikTok users reported finding creepy or paranormal things, including strange objects, eerie sounds, and even a suitcase containing human remains in Seattle. While some videos were staged, others fueled debates about the app's unsettling coincidences.

323. True

Open Water (2003) is based on the harrowing true story of Tom and Eileen Lonergan, who were accidentally left behind during a diving trip in the Great Barrier Reef in 1998. Despite extensive searches, the couple was never found, leading to speculation about their fate. The film captures the terror of isolation in open waters.

324. Unknown

Exploring the Unknown features urban explorers documenting eerie findings, from abandoned hospitals to desolate amusement parks. Episodes often capture mysterious noises, shadowy figures, and chilling atmospheres, making it a favorite among paranormal fans and adventurers.

325. D. 0010110

The YouTube channel *0010110* featured bizarre and disturbing videos of a masked figure performing strange rituals. The cryptic nature of the content, paired with clues hidden in the videos, led viewers to theorize about its meaning, from art project to genuine cries for help.

QUIZ

326. True or False: In 2022, a TikTok user claimed to document a "time loop," repeatedly encountering the same stranger at a coffee shop every day despite different times.

327. True or False: *Jaws* was the first film to be dubbed a "summer blockbuster."

328. True or False: The disappearance of Japan Airlines Flight 1628 over Alaska in 1986 remains one of the most mysterious UFO sightings.

329. A viral TikTok series featured a user hearing mysterious sounds behind a sealed _____ in their apartment.

330. What TikTok user sparked debates by claiming they captured footage of a "shadow person" in their basement?

    A. @GhostFinder
    B. @ShadowSeeker22
    C. @RealParanormalLife
    D. @BasementShadow

331. Who directed the meta-horror film *Scream*, which satirizes slasher movie clichés?

    A. Wes Craven
    B. John Carpenter
    C. Clive Barker
    D. Tobe Hooper

ANSWERS

326. True

A TikTok user shared videos of the same person always seated at the same coffee shop table, no matter the time or day. The videos sparked debates, with some suggesting it was evidence of a time loop or simulation glitch, while others called it a carefully staged hoax.

327. True

Jaws became the first true "summer blockbuster," with its release in June 1975. Its massive success, driven by innovative marketing, a nationwide release, and a thrilling premise, set the standard for high-grossing summer films and forever changed the way Hollywood approached major releases.

328. True

While Japan Airlines Flight 1628 did not disappear, the crew reported seeing UFOs while flying over Alaska in 1986. The incident involved radar anomalies and detailed descriptions of unidentified lights, making it one of the most documented and debated UFO sightings connected to Japan.

329. Door

The TikTok user discovered a door in their apartment that had been nailed shut and heard strange noises coming from behind it. Videos of their attempts to open the door revealed nothing unusual, but the eerie atmosphere left followers wondering if something paranormal was involved.

330. D. @BasementShadow

@BasementShadow posted videos of unexplained shadows moving across their basement walls, with no apparent source. The eerie clips gained millions of views, with some users calling it proof of shadow people and others suggesting clever editing.

331. A. Wes Craven

Wes Craven revitalized the slasher genre with *Scream*, introducing a self-aware script that both celebrated and critiqued horror tropes, featuring a mysterious killer known as Ghostface.

332. True or False: The Sphinx of Giza was once buried up to its neck in sand.

333. True or False: A Twitter thread in 2021 detailed a user's experience with a strange phone number that, when called, played disturbing sounds and cryptic messages.

334. In the movie *1408*, what is the significance of the room number?

    A. It's based on a real haunted hotel room.
    B. Adding the digits together equals the unlucky number 13.
    C. It's the same room number where a famous author died.
    D. It references the Bible verse Matthew 14:08.

335. Which horror movie is infamous for a series of unexplained tragedies, including multiple cast and crew deaths during and after production?

    A. The Exorcist
    B. Poltergeist
    C. The Omen
    D. Rosemary's Baby

336. True or False: During the filming of *The Exorcist*, the set of the MacNeil home caught fire, delaying production for six weeks.

337. The production of *The Omen* was plagued by accidents, including a plane crash, lightning strikes, and a zookeeper's death by _____.

ANSWERS

332. True

The Great Sphinx of Giza, one of Egypt's most iconic monuments, has been buried up to its neck in sand multiple times throughout history due to desert encroachment. It was fully excavated in the 20th century, revealing its lion body and enigmatic human face, which continues to inspire debate about its origins and purpose.

333. True

The user claimed to have found the number on a mysterious flyer and decided to call it. They recorded eerie static, distorted voices, and what sounded like screaming. The thread went viral, with theories ranging from ARGs (alternate reality games) to real-life creepiness.

334. B. Adding the digits together equals the unlucky number 13.

In *1408*, the titular hotel room is said to be cursed, with dozens of deaths occurring there over the years. The room number 1408 is significant because 1 + 4 + 0 + 8 equals 13, a number often associated with bad luck. This subtle detail adds to the eerie atmosphere of the film, which is based on a Stephen King short story.

335. B. Poltergeist

The *Poltergeist* series is infamous for its "curse," with several actors dying unexpectedly, including Heather O'Rourke, who played Carol Anne. Rumors also suggest that real skeletons were used in certain scenes, possibly contributing to the eerie misfortune surrounding the films.

336. True

A mysterious fire broke out on the set of *The Exorcist*, destroying most of the MacNeil home except for Regan's bedroom. Director William Friedkin believed the fire was a bad omen, and the crew brought a priest to bless the set before continuing filming.

337. Lions

During the filming of *The Omen*, the curse rumors intensified after a zookeeper working on set was killed by lions, and lightning struck planes carrying cast members. These incidents, coupled with eerie coincidences, solidified *The Omen* as one of Hollywood's most cursed productions.

QUIZ

338. What famous horror movie's lead actor reported strange occurrences, including hearing unexplained noises, after taking a prop home from set?

    A. The Conjuring
    B. The Amityville Horror
    C. Annabelle
    D. The Blair Witch Project

339. True or False: The set of *Rosemary's Baby* became infamous after its composer, Krzysztof Komeda, and producer William Castle experienced fatal or near-fatal illnesses during production.

340. While filming *Apocalypse Now*, the crew faced endless challenges, including a typhoon, Martin Sheen's heart attack, and the destruction of sets in the _____.

341. What 2005 horror remake had its lead actress reportedly experience supernatural events during production?

    A. The Amityville Horror
    B. The Ring
    C. The Grudge
    D. House of Wax

342. What eerie incident occurred during the filming of Alfred Hitchcock's *The Birds*, involving its lead actress Tippi Hedren?

    A. She was attacked by live birds during filming.
    B. She reported hearing strange whispers on set.
    C. A mirror shattered spontaneously in her dressing room.
    D. Hitchcock claimed the script was based on a real curse.

343. Where was Edgar Allan Poe born?

    A. Baltimore, Maryland
    B. Boston, Massachusetts
    C. Richmond, Virginia
    D. Philadelphia, Pennsylvania

ANSWERS

338. A. The Conjuring

Vera Farmiga, who played Lorraine Warren in *The Conjuring*, reported strange occurrences after filming, including unexplained claw marks appearing on her laptop. Many believe the eerie events were linked to the film's focus on real-life paranormal investigations.

339. True

During and after *Rosemary's Baby*, composer Krzysztof Komeda died of a brain injury, and producer William Castle suffered from severe health issues, including gallstones, leading him to believe the film was cursed. These tragedies added to the chilling legacy of this iconic horror film.

340. Philippines

Though not a horror film, *Apocalypse Now* has a reputation for being a cursed production. Filming in the Philippines was plagued by natural disasters, health emergencies, and extreme tension among the cast and crew, creating an atmosphere as chaotic as the story itself.

341. A. The Amityville Horror

While filming *The Amityville Horror* remake, Ryan Reynolds and Melissa George reported waking up at exactly 3:15 a.m., the supposed time of the original DeFeo murders. The eerie experiences left the cast and crew wondering if the set was truly haunted.

342. A. She was attacked by live birds during filming.

In *The Birds*, Hitchcock famously used live birds during several scenes, leading to terrifying moments for the cast, especially Tippi Hedren. In one harrowing instance, Hedren was attacked by birds thrown at her repeatedly by handlers, leaving her physically and emotionally shaken. Hitchcock's insistence on realism created an atmosphere of dread that spilled from the screen into real life.

343. B. Boston, Massachusetts

Edgar Allan Poe, often called the master of macabre, was born in Boston, Massachusetts, in 1809. Though he's closely associated with Baltimore, where he died mysteriously, Poe's birthplace reflects his early struggles before rising to literary fame.

QUIZ

344. True or False: H.P. Lovecraft died penniless and largely unrecognized for his work.

345. Mary Shelley wrote *Frankenstein* while staying near _____, Switzerland.

346. What tragic event in Bram Stoker's life may have influenced his writing of *Dracula*?

   A. His father's death from a mysterious illness
   B. His own near-fatal childhood illness
   C. His wife's betrayal
   D. His brother's disappearance

347. True or False: Stephen King survived a near-fatal car accident in 1999, which inspired elements of his later works.

348. Shirley Jackson, author of *The Haunting of Hill House*, was born in _____, California.

349. What unusual request did Franz Kafka make regarding his unpublished works before his death?

   A. He wanted them buried with him.
   B. He asked for them to be burned.
   C. He demanded they be hidden for 100 years.
   D. He instructed they be sold anonymously.

350. True or False: Anne Rice's New Orleans upbringing heavily influenced her *Vampire Chronicles* series.

ANSWERS

344. True

H.P. Lovecraft, the creator of the Cthulhu Mythos, died in poverty in 1937 from intestinal cancer. Despite his profound influence on horror fiction, he gained little recognition during his lifetime. Lovecraft's work achieved legendary status posthumously.

345. Lake Geneva

Mary Shelley conceived *Frankenstein* during a stormy summer at Lord Byron's villa near Lake Geneva in 1816. This gathering inspired one of the most enduring works of gothic horror, often called the first science fiction novel.

346. B. His own near-fatal childhood illness

Bram Stoker suffered a mysterious illness as a child that left him bedridden for years. This early brush with mortality likely influenced his fascination with life, death, and the supernatural, themes central to his masterpiece *Dracula*.

347. True

In 1999, Stephen King was struck by a van while walking along a road in Maine. The accident left him with severe injuries and inspired dark reflections in his writing, notably in *On Writing* and *Lisey's Story*.

348. San Francisco

Shirley Jackson, born in San Francisco in 1916, brought her keen observations of small-town life and human psychology into her chilling works. Her experiences with societal judgment and isolation influenced stories like *The Lottery* and *Hill House*.

349. B. He asked for them to be burned.

Franz Kafka, though not strictly a horror writer, infused his work with existential dread. Before his death, he asked his friend Max Brod to burn his unpublished manuscripts. Brod ignored the request, preserving classics like *The Trial* and *The Metamorphosis* for future generations.

350. True

Anne Rice's childhood in New Orleans, with its gothic architecture and rich history, deeply influenced her work. The city serves as the atmospheric backdrop for many of her *Vampire Chronicles* novels, including *Interview with the Vampire*.

QUIZ

351. What is one of the most popular theories about the purpose of Stonehenge?

A. It was a sacrificial altar for ancient druids.
B. It served as a prehistoric astronomical observatory.
C. It marked the burial site of legendary kings.
D. It was a natural phenomenon formed by glacial movement.

352. What chilling discovery was made in some of the burial sites at Machu Picchu?

A. Skeletons with signs of ritual decapitation
B. Bodies buried alive as offerings to the gods
C. Mass graves of sacrificed children
D. Remains of individuals with bound hands and feet

353. A viral Instagram story series claimed to document a "cursed _____" purchased from an antique store, leading to eerie events at the owner's home.

354. What Australian pilot disappeared in 1978 after reporting a UFO following his aircraft?

A. Frederick Valentich
B. Charles Kingsford Smith
C. Peter McCulloch
D. James Taylor

355. What horror anthology TV series featured an episode based on Clive Barker's *The Hellbound Heart*?

A. Tales from the Crypt
B. Masters of Horror
C. Night Gallery
D. Creepshow

356. In ancient Mesoamerican cultures like the Mayans, what was often used as the ball in ritual ball games?

A. A leather-wrapped stone
B. A human head
C. A carved wooden ball
D. A rubber ball

351. *B. It served as a prehistoric astronomical observatory.*

While the exact purpose of Stonehenge remains a mystery, one prevailing theory is that it was an astronomical observatory. The stones align with the solstices, suggesting it may have been used to track celestial events. Other theories range from its use as a burial ground to a site for religious ceremonies or healing rituals, adding to its enigmatic allure.

352. *B. Bodies buried alive as offerings to the gods*

Archaeological evidence suggests that some individuals may have been buried alive at Machu Picchu as part of Inca sacrificial rituals. The Incas believed such offerings were necessary to appease the gods and ensure the prosperity of their empire. This practice reflects the darker spiritual beliefs intertwined with the grandeur of the site.

353. *Doll*

The Instagram user posted photos and videos of a creepy doll that allegedly moved on its own and caused electronics to malfunction. Followers eagerly awaited updates, with many suggesting the doll should be returned to the store or burned to end its curse.

354. *A. Frederick Valentich*

Frederick Valentich disappeared while flying a small Cessna over the Bass Strait in Australia. Before vanishing, he radioed air traffic control to report a large, unidentified craft with bright lights hovering over him. His last transmission described the object as "hovering and not an aircraft." Neither Valentich nor his plane was ever found.

355. *B. Masters of Horror*

The Hellbound Heart, which inspired Barker's *Hellraiser,* was adapted for the *Masters of Horror* series in an episode called "Haeckel's Tale," bringing his dark vision to the small screen.

356. *B. A human head*

Some accounts suggest that after ritual sacrifices, the severed heads of captives were occasionally used as balls in ceremonial games, symbolizing cosmic struggles like life versus death or light versus dark.

QUIZ

357. The "Heretic's Fork" was a device designed to immobilize the _____ and prevent speaking.

358. Which American author, considered the father of modern horror, was born in Providence, Rhode Island, in 1890?

    A. Edgar Allan Poe
    B. H.P. Lovecraft
    C. Ambrose Bierce
    D. Nathaniel Hawthorne

359. Who played Dr. Hannibal Lecter in the NBC series *Hannibal*?

    A. Mads Mikkelsen
    B. Anthony Hopkins
    C. Hugh Dancy
    D. Laurence Fishburne

360. True or False: The practice of head shrinking (tsantsas) was used by the Jivaroan tribes of the Amazon to trap the soul of an enemy.

361. In *It* (2017), what object is associated with Pennywise the Dancing Clown?

    A. A red balloon
    B. A circus tent
    C. A carnival mask
    D. A yellow raincoat

362. What ghost is said to haunt the Château de Brissac in France?

    A. The White Lady
    B. The Grey Man
    C. The Green Lady
    D. The Bloody Countess

ANSWERS

357. Neck

The Heretic's Fork was a metal rod with prongs at either end, placed between the chin and chest or neck and collarbone. This cruel device prevented its victim from moving their head or speaking, symbolizing punishment for blasphemy or dissent.

358. B. H.P. Lovecraft

H.P. Lovecraft, born in Providence, Rhode Island, is best known for creating the Cthulhu Mythos and pioneering cosmic horror. His work often explored themes of forbidden knowledge and humanity's insignificance in the universe.

359. A. Mads Mikkelsen

Mads Mikkelsen brought a refined and chilling portrayal of Hannibal Lecter to the series, blending elegance with menace. His performance was praised for reinventing the character while respecting Thomas Harris' original creation.

360. True

The Jivaroan tribes believed shrinking an enemy's head prevented their soul from seeking vengeance. The process involved removing the skull, boiling the skin, and reshaping it to create a small, preserved trophy.

361. A. A red balloon

Pennywise's red balloon is a recurring symbol of his eerie presence, often appearing just before he strikes terror into his victims.

362. C. The Green Lady

The Château de Brissac is haunted by the spirit of Charlotte de Brézé, a noblewoman murdered by her husband after discovering her infidelity. Known as the "Green Lady" due to the green dress she reportedly wears, her ghost is said to wander the castle's halls. Visitors often report hearing her moaning in the night or catching glimpses of her disfigured face, which some say reflects the injuries she sustained during her death.

QUIZ

363. Clive Barker, author of *The Hellbound Heart* and creator of the *Hellraiser* series, was born in _____, England.

364. The practice of _____, or consuming parts of the dead, was used in some cultures as a way of honoring or gaining strength from the deceased.

365. Which novel by Shirley Jackson begins with the ominous line, "The villagers gathered in the square. . ."?

    A. The Haunting of Hill House
    B. We Have Always Lived in the Castle
    C. The Lottery
    D. Hangsaman

366. True or False: The Winchester Mystery House has staircases that lead to nowhere and doors that open into walls.

367. In Mary Shelley's *Frankenstein*, what is the name of Victor Frankenstein's best friend?

    A. Henry Clerval
    B. Robert Walton
    C. William Frankenstein
    D. Justine Moritz

368. What is the name of the 1982 horror film directed by John Carpenter that features a shape-shifting alien terrorizing an Antarctic research station?

    A. They Live
    B. The Thing
    C. Escape from New York
    D. Prince of Darkness

369. What year was the Salem Witch Trials, one of the most infamous events in American history?

    A. 1607
    B. 1620
    C. 1692
    D. 1711

ANSWERS

363. Liverpool

Clive Barker was born in Liverpool in 1952. His works often blend horror with dark fantasy, creating richly imaginative and macabre worlds.

364. Endocannibalism

Endocannibalism, practiced by groups like the Wari' of Brazil, involved eating the flesh of deceased family members as an act of reverence or mourning. It was seen as a way to spiritually connect with the dead.

365. C. The Lottery

Shirley Jackson's short story *The Lottery* shocked readers with its depiction of a ritualistic stoning in a small town. Its opening line establishes a deceptively peaceful setting before the chilling events unfold.

366. True

Sarah Winchester, heir to the Winchester rifle fortune, kept building her mansion in San Jose, California, for decades, believing it would confuse and trap the spirits of those killed by her family's rifles.

367. A. Henry Clerval

Henry Clerval is Victor's loyal and supportive friend. His tragic fate at the hands of Victor's creature underscores the consequences of Victor's hubris.

368. B. The Thing

The Thing is a remake of *The Thing from Another World* (1951) and is renowned for its groundbreaking practical effects and paranoid atmosphere. Though it initially underperformed at the box office, it has since been hailed as a sci-fi horror masterpiece.

369. C. 1692

The Salem Witch Trials occurred in 1692 in Massachusetts, leading to the execution of 20 people and the imprisonment of many others. This dark chapter in history remains a cautionary tale about mass hysteria and injustice.

QUIZ

370. What mysterious unsolved event in 1959 involved the deaths of nine hikers in Russia's Ural Mountains?

    A. The Tunguska Incident
    B. The Dyatlov Pass Incident
    C. The Siberian Shadows Mystery
    D. The Kolat Syakhl Enigma

371. What year did George A. Romero's *Night of the Living Dead* revolutionize the zombie genre?

    A. 1964
    B. 1968
    C. 1971
    D. 1974

372. True or False: Edgar Allan Poe's first published work was a poetry collection titled *Tamerlane and Other Poems.*

373. What ancient culture practiced live burial as a form of punishment for breaking religious vows?

    A. The Aztecs
    B. The Romans
    C. The Chinese
    D. The Egyptians

374. Which novel by Anne Rice begins with the line, "I see . . . I see ghosts"?

    A. Interview with the Vampire
    B. The Witching Hour
    C. The Vampire Lestat
    D. Queen of the Damned

375. What is the name of the ghost that haunts Luke Crain in *The Haunting of Hill House*?

    A. The Bent-Neck Lady
    B. The Tall Man
    C. The Screaming Woman
    D. The Smiling Ghost

ANSWERS

370. B. The Dyatlov Pass Incident

The Dyatlov Pass Incident remains one of the most chilling unsolved mysteries. The hikers were found dead under strange circumstances, including signs of massive internal injuries without external trauma, sparking theories of avalanches, military experiments, and even UFOs.

371. B. 1968

Night of the Living Dead (1968) introduced the modern concept of zombies as flesh-eating ghouls. Romero's film also broke ground by casting Duane Jones, a Black actor, in the lead role, adding layers of social commentary to the horror.

372. True

Poe's *Tamerlane and Other Poems* was published anonymously in 1827. Though it received little attention at the time, Poe went on to revolutionize horror and detective fiction with works like *The Tell-Tale Heart* and *The Raven*.

373. B. The Romans

In Rome, Vestal Virgins who broke their vows of chastity were sometimes buried alive, a punishment meant to placate the gods and maintain the sanctity of their temple.

374. B. The Witching Hour

The Witching Hour, the first book in Anne Rice's Mayfair Witches series, blends gothic horror with themes of witchcraft, family legacies, and the supernatural. It solidified Rice's place as a master of atmospheric storytelling.

375. B. The Tall Man

The Tall Man is a terrifying figure with an unnaturally long stature and a floating gait, representing one of the many psychological and supernatural horrors faced by the Crain family.

376. _____ is the term used to describe a ghost or spirit that appears to warn of impending death or danger.

377. What haunting phenomenon was reported by survivors in the hardest-hit areas after the 2004 tsunami?

   A. Ghostly figures searching for their families
   B. Sounds of crying and wailing near the shore at night
   C. Unexplained footprints leading to the sea
   D. All of the above

378. Which legendary horror actor, known for playing Count Dracula in Hammer films, portrayed the corrupted wizard Saruman in *The Lord of the Rings* trilogy?

   A. Peter Cushing
   B. Vincent Price
   C. Christopher Lee
   D. Ian Holm

379. What is the name of the protagonist in Bram Stoker's *Dracula* who travels to Transylvania to meet Count Dracula?

   A. Jonathan Harker
   B. Abraham Van Helsing
   C. Renfield
   D. Arthur Holmwood

380. What is the mysterious "angel" in *Midnight Mass* revealed to be?

   A. A demon
   B. A vampire
   C. A fallen saint
   D. A hallucination

381. Bram Stoker, the author of *Dracula*, was born in _____, Ireland, in 1847.

ANSWERS

376. Banshee

In Irish folklore, a banshee is a female spirit whose mournful wail signals death in a family. Stories of banshees have been passed down for centuries, adding to the rich tapestry of Celtic myths.

377. D. All of the above

Survivors and locals in areas like Thailand and Sri Lanka reported seeing ghostly figures and hearing cries at night. Many believed these were spirits of those who perished in the disaster, still searching for loved ones or struggling to find peace.

378. C. Christopher Lee

Christopher Lee was the *only* cast member of *The Lord of the Rings* who had actually met J.R.R. Tolkien in real life—he read the books once every year and *begged* to play Gandalf. Instead, director Peter Jackson cast him as Saruman the White, whose descent into evil was perfectly matched by Lee's imposing voice and stare. He brought a lifetime of horror gravitas to the role, proving once again that evil in fantasy is just horror in disguise—with better hair. And yes, he reportedly corrected Peter Jackson on Tolkien pronunciation. Respect.

379.. A. Jonathan Harker

Jonathan Harker is a solicitor who travels to Dracula's castle, unknowingly stepping into a nightmare of vampires and ancient evil.

380. B. A vampire

The "angel" in *Midnight Mass* is a vampire-like creature that feeds on blood and spreads its curse through the community under the guise of religious salvation. Its ambiguous nature deepens the show's exploration of faith and morality.

381. Dublin

Bram Stoker's *Dracula*, published in 1897, defined the modern vampire mythos. Born in Dublin, Ireland, Stoker worked as a theater manager before achieving literary fame with his gothic masterpiece.

QUIZ

382. True or False: In the Mayan ritual known as the *sacred cenote*, victims were thrown into a water-filled sinkhole as offerings to the gods.

383. True or False: The legend of the Bell Witch is considered one of America's most documented hauntings.

384. Which terrifying clown-faced character made Sid Haig a cult horror legend in Rob Zombie's films?

    A. Captain Slaughter
    B. Sheriff Wydell
    C. Uncle Deadly
    D. Captain Spaulding

385. Which family claimed to have been attacked by small, glowing "goblins" at their farmhouse in Kentucky in 1955?

    A. The Hopkins family
    B. The Sutton family
    C. The Walton family
    D. The Hill family

386. In Anne Rice's *Interview with the Vampire*, what is the name of the child vampire Louis and Lestat care for?

    A. Claudia
    B. Madeleine
    C. Marguerite
    D. Elise

387. True or False: The Chupacabra, a creature from Latin American folklore, is believed to eat livestock

ANSWERS

382. True

The Mayans believed cenotes were portals to the underworld and used them for human sacrifices. Archaeological dives have uncovered bones and artifacts at the bottom of these sacred sinkholes.

383. True

The Bell Witch legend from Adams, Tennessee, dates back to the early 19th century. The spirit reportedly tormented the Bell family with unexplained sounds, physical attacks, and eerie messages. The story has been retold in books, films, and documentaries.

384. D. Captain Spaulding

Sid Haig cemented his place in horror history with his unforgettable performance as Captain Spaulding, the twisted, foul-mouthed, chicken-loving clown from Rob Zombie's *House of 1000 Corpses* (2003), *The Devil's Rejects* (2005), and *3 from Hell* (2019). Part menace, part dark comedy, Spaulding was as unpredictable as he was grotesquely charismatic—Haig's portrayal made him an instant icon in the world of extreme horror. Though he passed away in 2019, Sid Haig's deranged smile still haunts the genre.

385. B. The Sutton family

The Sutton family and their guests described being terrorized by small, silver-skinned creatures with large ears and glowing eyes near Kelly, Kentucky. The creatures reportedly floated and were resistant to gunfire. This bizarre encounter became a cornerstone of UFO lore and inspired the phrase "little green men."

386. A. Claudia

Claudia is turned into a vampire as a child and becomes one of the novel's most tragic figures, trapped forever in a child's body.

387. False

The Chupacabra, first reported in Puerto Rico in the 1990s, is described as a reptilian or dog-like creature. Its name means "goat-sucker" in Spanish, and it is said to kill livestock by draining their blood through puncture wounds.

QUIZ

388. In Filipino folklore, the _____ is a vampiric creature that splits its body in half and flies at night to prey on pregnant women.

389. What creature from Scottish folklore is said to haunt rivers and lakes, dragging unsuspecting victims to their watery deaths?

   A. Kelpie
   B. Selkie
   C. Banshee
   D. Dullahan

390. Which creature from West African folklore is a shape-shifting trickster who often takes the form of a spider?

   A. Anansi
   B. Mami Wata
   C. Aswang
   D. Sasabonsam

391. In *The Exorcist* by William Peter Blatty, the possessed girl's name is _____.

392. What is the name of the vengeful ghost in Mexican folklore who is said to cry out for her lost children?

   A. La Llorona
   B. El Cucuy
   C. La Bruja
   D. El Silbón

393. True or False: The Wendigo, a creature from Indigenous North American folklore, represents greed, cannibalism, and unending hunger.

394. What chilling discovery was made by rescue workers in the aftermath of the 2004 tsunami?

   A. A ship stranded in the middle of a city
   B. An entire village wiped away with no trace of its residents
   C. Thousands of personal belongings scattered far inland
   D. All of the above

ANSWERS

388. Manananggal

The Manananggal is a horrifying creature from Filipino folklore. By severing its upper body and sprouting bat-like wings, it preys on the unborn, using a long, tube-like tongue to drain the fetus's blood. Protection includes salt or garlic placed on its lower body.

389. A. Kelpie

Kelpies are water spirits that can shape-shift into horses or humans. They often lure people into riding them, only to dive into the water and drown their victims. The legend reflects the dangers of unpredictable waters in Scottish lore.

390. A. Anansi

Anansi is a beloved figure in West African folklore and is often portrayed as a cunning spider. While usually a trickster, Anansi's stories also teach valuable lessons about wisdom and resourcefulness, blending humor with myth.

391. Regan

Regan MacNeil is the young girl possessed by a demonic entity in *The Exorcist*, setting the stage for one of the most famous exorcism stories in horror history.

392. A. La Llorona

La Llorona, or "The Weeping Woman," is a tragic figure in Mexican folklore who drowned her children in a fit of rage and now wanders rivers and lakes, wailing in sorrow. Her eerie cries are said to forewarn death or misfortune.

393. True

The Wendigo is a terrifying creature associated with cold, famine, and greed. According to Algonquin legend, humans who resort to cannibalism may transform into Wendigos, forever cursed to wander in search of human flesh.

394. D. All of the above

The tsunami's devastating force stranded ships miles inland, erased entire communities, and spread personal belongings over vast areas. These surreal sights underscored the disaster's scale and power, leaving survivors and rescue workers haunted.

QUIZ

395. What was the first major work published by Richard Matheson, the author of *I Am Legend*?

   A. Hell House
   B. I Am Legend
   C. Born of Man and Woman
   D. The Shrinking Man

396. What is the name of the alien corporation in *Aliens* (1986) that tries to bring the xenomorphs back to Earth?

   A. Tyrell Corporation
   B. Weyland-Yutani
   C. Cyberdyne Systems
   D. OmniCorp

397. In Romanian folklore, what was the name of the vampire-like creature believed to rise from the grave to drink blood?

   A. Strigoi
   B. Moroi
   C. Nosferatu
   D. Vampyr

398. In Chinese folklore, a _____ is the spirit of a deceased person that returns to seek revenge or fulfill unfinished business.

399. What creature terrorizes the characters in Richard Matheson's *I Am Legend*?

   A. Vampires
   B. Zombies
   C. Werewolves
   D. Ghosts

400. What eerie contraption was known as the "Murderer's Chair" in 18th-century Europe?

   A. A spiked execution chair
   B. A chair designed to drown its occupant
   C. A chair that electrocuted people
   D. A chair with retractable blades

ANSWERS

395. C. Born of Man and Woman

Matheson's short story *Born of Man and Woman* (1950) launched his career as a speculative fiction writer. His novel *I Am Legend* remains one of the most influential works in the horror and science fiction genres.

396. B. Weyland-Yutani

The Weyland-Yutani Corporation's motto, "Building better worlds," is dripping with irony given their reckless pursuit of the deadly xenomorph species.

397. A. Strigoi

Strigoi are undead spirits or reanimated corpses that feed on the blood of the living. They were feared for their ability to shapeshift, control the weather, and torment their families.

398. Hungry Ghost

The Hungry Ghost is a common figure in Chinese folklore, representing souls who died violently, were neglected, or left unresolved matters. Offerings are made during the Ghost Festival to appease them and prevent misfortune.

399. A. Vampires

The "infected" in *I Am Legend* are vampiric creatures, though they have been reinterpreted as zombies in some adaptations. Matheson's novel helped define modern post-apocalyptic horror.

400. A. A spiked execution chair

The "Murderer's Chair" was a spiked metal seat used for torture and execution. Victims would bleed to death while seated, and the design ensured no part of the body escaped the pain.

QUIZ

401. What 2018 horror film by Ari Aster begins with a devastating family tragedy and evolves into a chilling tale of a demonic cult?

    A. Midsommar
    B. Hereditary
    C. The Witch
    D. The Lodge

402. True or False: Jordan Peele's *Get Out* (2017) won the Academy Award for Best Picture.

403. In *A Quiet Place* (2018), the characters must live in near silence to avoid being hunted by _____.

404. What group is believed to have mummified their dead using smoke instead of desiccation or chemicals?

    A. The Egyptians
    B. The Chinchorro
    C. The Torajans
    D. The Zoroastrians

405. What 2019 folk horror film directed by Ari Aster takes place during a pagan festival in Sweden?

    A. The Wicker Man
    B. Midsommar
    C. The Ritual
    D. The Lighthouse

406. What is the name of the parallel dimension in *Stranger Things*?

    A. The Other Side
    B. The Upside Down
    C. The Shadow World
    D. The Nether Zone

401. B. Hereditary

Hereditary explores themes of grief, family dysfunction, and the supernatural, earning acclaim for its unsettling atmosphere and Toni Collette's standout performance. It's often regarded as one of the most terrifying films of the decade.

402. False

While *Get Out* didn't win Best Picture, it earned Jordan Peele the Academy Award for Best Original Screenplay. The film's sharp commentary on race and social issues, combined with its horror elements, made it a groundbreaking success.

403. Blind monsters with acute hearing

John Krasinski's *A Quiet Place* captivated audiences with its unique premise and tense atmosphere. The film's use of sound—or lack thereof—created a nerve-wracking experience that redefined modern creature horror.

404. C. The Torajans

The Torajan people of Indonesia practiced unique mummification techniques, including smoking the body to preserve it for years. They continue to honor their dead with elaborate rituals.

405. B. Midsommar

Midsommar follows a group of friends who attend a midsummer festival in a remote Swedish village, only to become entangled in the community's bizarre and sinister rituals. Its bright, daylight aesthetic contrasts with its dark themes of grief and cults.

406. B. The Upside Down

The Upside Down is a dark, monstrous mirror of reality that serves as the source of many of the show's terrors, including the Demogorgon and the Mind Flayer.

QUIZ

407. With the 2015 Nepal earthquake, what was discovered beneath Kathmandu's Swayambhunath Stupa after it was damaged by the earthquake?

    A. A hidden chamber containing ancient relics
    B. Undeciphered scrolls written in Sanskrit
    C. Fossilized remains of early settlers
    D. A buried shrine thought to be lost

408. True or False: Romanian villagers believed that garlic could ward off vampires.

409. In Thomas Harris' *The Silence of the Lambs*, what does Hannibal Lecter famously request from Clarice Starling?

    A. A bottle of Chianti
    B. A quid pro quo
    C. An old case file
    D. A pen and paper

410. True or False: After the 2011 earthquake and tsunami in Japan, many taxi drivers in affected areas reported picking up "ghost passengers."

ANSWERS

407. A. A hidden chamber containing ancient relics

Restoration efforts after the quake revealed a hidden chamber beneath the Swayambhunath Stupa (also known as the Monkey Temple). Inside, workers found ancient relics, adding to the site's mystique and significance in Buddhist tradition.

408. True

Garlic was one of the most popular protections against strigoi in Romanian folklore. People would hang it over doors, windows, and even rub it on themselves to keep vampires at bay.

409. B. A quid pro quo

Hannibal Lecter offers Clarice insights into a serial killer in exchange for personal details about her life, creating one of fiction's most iconic and chilling dynamics.

410. True

In towns like Ishinomaki, taxi drivers reported encounters with ghostly passengers who vanished mid-ride. These stories often involved people asking to be taken to places destroyed by the tsunami. Many believe these sightings were spirits of those who perished, seeking closure.

QUIZ

411. In *Pet Sematary* by Stephen King, what is the name of the family cat that is brought back to life?

    A. Tiger
    B. Winston
    C. Church
    D. Salem

412. Which 2020 horror-comedy stars Samara Weaving as a newlywed who becomes the target of a deadly family ritual?

    A. Ready or Not
    B. The Hunt
    C. The Babysitter
    D. Happy Death Day

413. In *Friday the 13th* (1980), who is revealed to be the killer?

    A. Jason Voorhees
    B. Pamela Voorhees
    C. Ralph the Crazy Townsperson
    D. Alice Hardy

414. To prevent a strigoi from rising, villagers would often drive a wooden _____ into the corpse's chest.

415. What couple claimed to have been abducted by aliens in New Hampshire in 1961?

    A. Barney and Betty Hill
    B. Travis and Linda Walton
    C. Richard and Joyce Healy
    D. George and Kathy Lutz

416. True or False: The horror film *The Lighthouse* (2019) was shot in color but digitally altered to black and white for effect.

417. In *Dr. Jekyll and Mr. Hyde* by Robert Louis Stevenson, what potion ingredient allows Dr. Jekyll to transform into Mr. Hyde?

    A. A rare flower extract
    B. A mysterious salt
    C. Distilled mercury
    D. Dragon's blood

411. C. Church

Church, short for Winston Churchill, is the Creed family's pet cat that is resurrected in the sinister burial ground behind their house, bringing dread with him.

412. A. Ready or Not

Ready or Not follows Grace, a bride who discovers her new in-laws are playing a deadly game of hide-and-seek. The film balances humor, gore, and social commentary, making it a standout in the horror-comedy genre.

413. B. Pamela Voorhees

Jason Voorhees doesn't become the franchise's iconic slasher until later films. In the original, it's his mother, Pamela Voorhees, who commits the murders as revenge for her son's drowning.

414. Stake

The wooden stake, often made of ash or hawthorn, was a common method used to pin strigoi to their graves, ensuring they could not rise and harm the living.

415. A. Barney and Betty Hill

Barney and Betty Hill were driving home when they encountered a UFO. Under hypnosis, they later recounted being taken aboard the craft and subjected to medical examinations. Their story is one of the first widely reported alien abduction cases and remains a cornerstone of UFO folklore.

416. False

The Lighthouse was shot entirely in black and white using vintage equipment to create an authentic and eerie atmosphere. The film's unsettling story of two lighthouse keepers descending into madness earned critical acclaim.

417. B. A mysterious salt

The transformation relies on a special salt, which later becomes unavailable, trapping Jekyll in his monstrous duality.

418. What 2022 horror film directed by Ti West is set on a rural farm and features an aspiring group of adult filmmakers being hunted?

    A. Fresh
    B. X
    C. Nope
    D. Smile

419. What unusual burial practice was sometimes performed in Romania to prevent vampirism?

    A. Burying the corpse face down
    B. Cutting off the head
    C. Placing a brick in the corpse's mouth
    D. All of the above

420. In Jordan Peele's *Nope* (2022), the mysterious UFO is revealed to be a _____.

421. True or False: The brazen bull was a torture device designed to roast victims alive inside a hollow, bull-shaped container.

422. Which actress delivered the first spoken lines in the 1931 film *Dracula* but was not widely credited for her role?

    A. Gloria Stuart
    B. Carla Laemmle
    C. Helen Chandler
    D. Lupita Tovar

423. The central haunting in *The Amityville Horror* is said to have been caused by _____.

424. What gruesome device was used in colonial America to punish gossips and scolds?

    A. The Scold's Bridle
    B. The Ducking Stool
    C. The Stocks
    D. All of the above

418. B. X

X is a homage to 70s slasher films, following a group of young filmmakers who rent a remote farm to shoot an adult film. When the elderly hosts discover their plans, the weekend turns into a bloodbath.

419. D. All of the above

These methods were believed to confuse or incapacitate strigoi. Burying the corpse face down was thought to make them dig deeper into the earth rather than rise from the grave.

420. Living creature

Jordan Peele's *Nope* reimagines the UFO as a predatory, living creature. The film blends horror, sci-fi, and social commentary, exploring themes of exploitation and spectacle in a way that challenges genre conventions.

421. True

The brazen bull was an ancient Greek device used to execute prisoners. Victims were locked inside, and a fire was lit beneath the bull, heating it until the person was roasted alive. The screams were said to sound like a bull roaring, thanks to specially designed vents.

422. B. Carla Laemmle

Carla Laemmle, niece of Universal Pictures founder Carl Laemmle, had a small part in the opening scene of *Dracula*, playing a passenger reading from a travel guide. Despite her contribution, her role went uncredited, reflecting the common practice of the time to overlook minor actors. Carla became a beloved figure in horror history, later sharing memories of working on the film.

423. A mass murder

The house in *The Amityville Horror* is infamous for its history of violence. The real-life DeFeo family murders served as the basis for the chilling events depicted in the book.

424. D. All of the above

Punishments for gossip or nagging in colonial America were often designed to humiliate the victim. The Scold's Bridle was a metal mask with a tongue depressor, the Ducking Stool involved public dunking in water, and the Stocks restrained people for public ridicule.

QUIZ

425. True or False: The skeletons in the pool scene of *Poltergeist* (1982) were real human skeletons.

426. True or False: During the filming of *Rosemary's Baby* (1968), composer Krzysztof Komeda died under mysterious circumstances shortly after the film wrapped.

427. What Edgar Allan Poe story involves a man sealing his victim inside a wall?

   A. The Tell-Tale Heart
   B. The Fall of the House of Usher
   C. The Cask of Amontillado
   D. The Black Cat

428. The Aztecs practiced _____ sacrifice to ensure the sun would continue to rise.

429. True or False: Strigoi were believed to leave their graves at night to attend dances or feasts in their villages.

430. What disturbing fact about the set of *A Nightmare on Elm Street* (1984) added to its creepy atmosphere?

   A. The boiler room scenes were shot in a real abandoned asylum.
   B. The house used in the film had a history of hauntings.
   C. The crew experienced multiple electrical malfunctions during key scenes.
   D. The street where it was filmed had a series of unsolved murders.

431. What was the primary cause of death during the Black Death in the 14th century?

   A. Starvation
   B. Bubonic plague spread by fleas
   C. Warfare
   D. Religious persecution

ANSWERS

425.True

In *Poltergeist*, the crew used real human skeletons in the pool scene because they were cheaper than plastic replicas. Actress JoBeth Williams later revealed she was unaware of this during filming, and the revelation added to the film's eerie reputation.

426. True

Krzysztof Komeda, who composed the haunting score for *Rosemary's Baby*, died shortly after completing the film due to a head injury. His death, along with other tragedies connected to the production, led to speculation about a curse surrounding the movie.

427. C. The Cask of Amontillado

In this macabre tale of revenge, Montresor lures Fortunato into the catacombs with promises of fine wine before sealing him alive behind a wall.

428. Human

The Aztecs believed human sacrifice was necessary to sustain the gods and keep the universe in balance. Hearts were often removed from live victims as offerings to the sun god.

429. True

Strigoi were thought to be highly social in death, sometimes reuniting with family or attending gatherings. However, their presence brought misfortune and death to those they visited.

430. A. The boiler room scenes were shot in a real abandoned asylum.

The eerie boiler room scenes in *A Nightmare on Elm Street* were filmed in an abandoned asylum, adding a layer of authentic dread to the production. The location's unsettling history and atmosphere enhanced the film's terrifying visuals.

431. B. Bubonic plague spread by fleas

The Black Death killed an estimated 25 million people in Europe, with the disease spread by fleas carried on rats. Symptoms included swollen lymph nodes, fever, and a high mortality rate. The plague's impact on society and culture was profound, and it remains a haunting chapter of history.

QUIZ

432. The Rack, a device used during the Spanish Inquisition, stretched a victim's _____ to cause excruciating pain.

433. True or False: The Monte Cristo Homestead in Australia is said to be haunted by the ghost of a maid who fell to her death down a staircase.

434. The Hill of Crosses in _____ is a site where thousands of crosses have been placed, creating a surreal and eerie landscape.

435. What is the nickname for the zombies in *The Walking Dead*?

   A. Walkers
   B. Creepers
   C. Biters
   D. Roamers

436. What ancient practice involved placing a heavy stone or rock on a condemned person's chest until they confessed or died?

   A. The Blood Eagle
   B. Scaphism
   C. Pressing
   D. Crushing

437. What medieval device was used to crush the fingers of prisoners?

   A. The Thumbscrew
   B. The Iron Claw
   C. The Torturer's Vice
   D. The Bone Grinder

438. In *Scream* (1996), what rule does Randy say you must never break in order to survive a horror movie?

   A. Never split up.
   B. Never say, "I'll be right back."
   C. Never answer the phone.
   D. Never turn your back on the killer.

ANSWERS

432. Limbs

The Rack was a torture device where victims were tied by their wrists and ankles and slowly stretched, often dislocating joints and tearing muscles. It was infamous for its use in extracting confessions.

433. True

The Monte Cristo Homestead, regarded as Australia's most haunted house, has a dark history of violent deaths, including a maid who fell—or was pushed—down the staircase. Her spirit is said to linger, along with others who met tragic ends on the property.

434. Lithuania

The Hill of Crosses in Lithuania is a hauntingly beautiful pilgrimage site where visitors have placed thousands of crosses over centuries. Despite being destroyed multiple times, locals have continuously rebuilt it, believing the site holds spiritual power.

435. A. Walkers

The term "walkers" is commonly used in the series to describe the undead. Different communities adopt their own nicknames, reflecting their isolation and unique survival methods.

436. C. Pressing

Pressing, or "peine forte et dure," was used in medieval Europe as a form of torture or execution. It was famously used on Giles Corey during the Salem Witch Trials.

437. A. The Thumbscrew

The Thumbscrew was a small but cruel device that applied intense pressure to the fingers or thumbs, causing severe pain and often breaking bones. It was frequently used to extract confessions.

438. B. Never say, "I'll be right back."

Randy's "rules for surviving a horror movie" add meta humor to *Scream*, poking fun at the genre's well-worn clichés.

439. True or False: The Voynich Manuscript has been successfully decoded and is now understood to be an elaborate medieval herbal guide.

440. Mary King's Close in Edinburgh is said to be haunted by _____, a child ghost who seeks her lost doll.

441. What was a common way to identify a vampire in Romanian villages?

    A. A corpse with long fingernails
    B A body that didn't decompose
    C. A corpse with blood around its mouth
    D. All of the above

442. What object, sold on eBay in the early 2000s, is believed to house a malicious spirit?

    A. The Dybbuk Box
    B. Robert the Doll
    C. The Crying Boy Painting
    D. The Weeping Mirror

443. In *The Stand* by Stephen King, what is the name of the mysterious antagonist also known as "The Dark Man"?

    A. Randall Flagg
    B. The Man in Black
    C. The Crimson King
    D. Leland Gaunt

444. Which island near Venice is considered one of the most haunted places in the world due to its history as a quarantine station and mental asylum?

    A. Poveglia Island
    B. San Michele Island
    C. Murano Island
    D. Burano Island

445. Which literary character does Eva Green's character, Vanessa Ives, face off against in *Penny Dreadful*?

    A. Dracula
    B. Dr. Jekyll
    C. The Invisible Man
    D. Frankenstein's Monster

ANSWERS

439. False

The Voynich Manuscript remains one of history's great unsolved mysteries. Written in an unknown script and language, it contains strange botanical illustrations and diagrams. Despite extensive research, its origins and purpose are still unknown.

440. Annie

Mary King's Close is an underground street in Edinburgh where many died during the plague. Annie, the ghost of a young girl, is one of its most famous hauntings. Visitors often leave dolls and toys for her, adding to the eerie atmosphere.

441. D. All of the above

If a corpse exhibited these signs during exhumation, it was considered proof of vampirism. Rituals would then be performed to destroy the vampire and protect the village.

442. A. The Dybbuk Box

The Dybbuk Box is a wine cabinet said to contain a malevolent spirit from Jewish folklore. After being sold on eBay, it became infamous for bringing misfortune to its owners, inspiring the horror movie *The Possession*.

443. A. Randall Flagg

Randall Flagg is a recurring villain in King's works, representing chaos and evil. In *The Stand*, he leads the forces of darkness in the post-apocalyptic battle.

444. A. Poveglia Island

Poveglia Island was used to quarantine plague victims and later as a mental asylum. Thousands died there under horrific conditions, and locals claim the spirits of the dead still haunt the island, making it a place few dare to visit.

445. A. Dracula

Vanessa Ives confronts Dracula in *Penny Dreadful*, blending gothic horror and literary lore with her struggle against the supernatural forces trying to claim her soul.

446. True or False: The "Garrote" was used as a method of execution by strangulation in Spain until the late 1970s.

447. True or False: Tibetan sky burials involve leaving a body exposed for vultures as a form of burial.

448. What mysterious event in 1959 involved the unexplained deaths of nine hikers in the Ural Mountains?

   A. The Tunguska Event
   B. The Dyatlov Pass Incident
   C. The Kholat Syakhl Mystery
   D. The Yeti Encounter

449. What nickname is given to Chillingham Castle in England, known for its history of torture and reported hauntings?

   A. The Ghost Castle
   B. The Witch's Fortress
   C. The Haunted Heart of Northumberland
   D. The Bloodiest Castle in Britain

450. True or False: Guillermo del Toro personally directed all the episodes of *Cabinet of Curiosities*.

451. What creatures terrorize the group of women in *The Descent*?

   A. Bats
   B. Humanoid cave dwellers
   C. Giant spiders
   D. Rabid wolves

452. In *The Woman in Black* by Susan Hill, what tragic event fuels the ghost's vengeance?

   A. Her death during childbirth
   B. The drowning of her child
   C. Being betrayed by her lover
   D. Her murder by a sibling

ANSWERS

446. True

The Garrote was a device used to execute prisoners by tightening a metal collar around their necks, either strangling them or breaking their spinal cord. Its last known use in Spain was in 1974, making it one of the more recent examples of such a brutal method.

447. True

Sky burials are a traditional Tibetan practice where the body is offered to vultures, symbolizing the impermanence of life and serving as a final act of generosity.

448. B. The Dyatlov Pass Incident

While not explicitly an alien encounter, the Dyatlov Pass Incident has been linked to UFO theories. The hikers were found dead under bizarre circumstances, including radiation exposure, missing body parts, and strange injuries. Some reports suggest strange lights were seen in the sky near the site.

449. D. The Bloodiest Castle in Britain

Chillingham Castle earned its reputation due to its gruesome history, including a torture chamber and countless ghost sightings. Visitors report eerie sounds, sudden cold spots, and even ghostly apparitions wandering the halls.

450. False

While Guillermo del Toro curated and introduced each story, the episodes were directed by a variety of acclaimed filmmakers, including Jennifer Kent (*The Babadook*) and Panos Cosmatos (*Mandy*).

451. B. Humanoid cave dwellers

The cave creatures in *The Descent*, known as Crawlers, are blind, feral humanoids adapted to life in the dark. Their sudden, violent appearances heighten the claustrophobic tension in the film.

452. B. The drowning of her child

The Woman in Black, Jennet Humfrye, seeks revenge for the death of her son, who drowned after being taken away from her, making her haunting deeply personal and tragic.

QUIZ

453. Which horror icon, famous for playing Frankenstein's Monster, was actually born as William Henry Pratt?

   A. Lon Chaney
   B. Vincent Price
   C. Bela Lugosi
   D. Boris Karloff

454. What was the name of the Romanian holiday associated with protecting oneself from strigoi?

   A. St. Andrew's Eve
   B. The Night of the Dead
   C. Walpurgisnacht
   D. All Souls' Day

455. What invention was developed in the 19th century to prevent premature burial?

   A. A bell attached to a coffin
   B. A spring-loaded coffin lid
   C. An air vent with a flag
   D. A motion-detecting device

456. True or False: Leap Castle in Ireland is said to be haunted by an elemental spirit with a foul odor and a deformed appearance.

457. How was George A. Romero's *Night of the Living Dead* (1968) primarily funded?

   A. A government arts grant
   B. A group of local investors
   C. Romero's personal savings
   D. A major studio's low-budget division

458. What was the purpose of the ancient Irish practice of *bog burial*?

   A. Honoring tribal leaders
   B. Sacrificing to fertility gods
   C. Punishing criminals
   D. Preserving remains for the afterlife

ANSWERS

453. D. Boris Karloff

Karloff adopted his stage name early in his acting career, worried that his family might disapprove of his life on stage. He wasn't just Frankenstein's Monster—he also starred in *The Mummy* (1932), *Black Sabbath* (1963), and even voiced the Grinch in the 1966 animated classic. Talk about range: from undead to Whoville.

454. A. St. Andrew's Eve

St. Andrew's Eve (November 29) was believed to be a time when strigoi were especially active. People would stay indoors, rub garlic on doors and windows, and light candles to ward off evil spirits.

455. A. A bell attached to a coffin

Known as "safety coffins," these devices included bells or flags to signal if a person buried alive managed to awaken. These inventions arose due to fears of premature burial during cholera outbreaks and other illnesses.

456. True

Leap Castle is home to the mysterious "Elemental," a spirit said to be associated with the castle's violent past. Its appearance and foul smell are believed to signal danger or foretell disaster.

457. B. A group of local investors, including dentists

Night of the Living Dead was funded with about $114,000, much of which came from local investors in Pittsburgh. Surprisingly, many of these investors were dentists who believed in Romero's vision and wanted to support local filmmaking. The film's shoestring budget didn't hinder its creativity, as it became a groundbreaking classic that earned millions and revolutionized the horror genre.

458. B. Sacrificing to fertility gods

Bog bodies found in Ireland are believed to have been sacrifices to gods, often for fertility or agricultural success. The anaerobic conditions of the bogs preserved the bodies remarkably well.

QUIZ

459. Which iconic role did Bela Lugosi famously portray in the 1931 Universal Pictures classic that forever typecast him in horror cinema?

   A. Frankenstein's Monster
   B. The Mummy
   C. Count Dracula
   D. The Wolf Man

ANSWERS

459. C. Count Dracula

Bela Lugosi *was* Dracula. His thick Hungarian accent, piercing stare, and theatrical flair brought Bram Stoker's vampire to life in ways that still influence the undead today. But the role was both a blessing and a curse—Lugosi was so closely identified with the Count that he struggled to find work outside the horror genre. He was even buried in his Dracula cape.

THE END?

Not if you want to dive into more of Crystal Lake Publishing's Tales from the Darkest Depths!

Check out our amazing website and online store or download our latest catalog here.
https://geni.us/CLPCatalog

We always have great new projects and content on the website to dive into, as well as a newsletter, behind the scenes options, social media platforms, our own dark fiction shared-world series and our very own webstore. Our webstore even has categories specifically for KU books, non-fiction, anthologies, and of course more novels and novellas.

Readers. . .

Thank you for reading *Test Your Terror*. We hope you enjoyed this quiz book. If you have a moment, please review *Test Your Terror* at the store where you bought it.

Help other readers by telling them why you enjoyed this book. No need to write an in-depth discussion. Even a single sentence will be greatly appreciated. Reviews go a long way to helping a book sell, and is great for an author's career. It'll also help us to continue publishing quality books.

Thank you again for taking the time to journey with Crystal Lake Publishing.

You will find links to all our social media platforms on our Linktree page.
https://linktr.ee/CrystalLakePublishing

Follow us on Amazon:

MISSION STATEMENT

Since its founding in August 2012, Crystal Lake has quickly become one of the world's leading publishers of Dark Fiction and Horror books. In 2023, Crystal Lake officially transitioned into an entertainment company, joining several other divisions, genres, and imprints, including Torrid Waters, Crystal Lake Comics, Crystal Lake Games, Crystal Lake Kids, and many more.

While we strive to present only the highest quality fiction and entertainment, we also endeavour to support authors along their writing journey. We offer our time and experience in non-fiction projects, as well as author mentoring and services, at competitive prices.

With several Bram Stoker Award wins and many other wins and nominations (including the HWA's Specialty Press Award), Crystal Lake Publishing puts integrity, honor, and respect at the forefront of our publishing operations.

We strive for each book and outreach program we spearhead to not only entertain and touch or comment on issues that affect our readers, but also to strengthen and support the Dark Fiction field and its authors.

Not only do we find and publish authors we believe are destined for greatness, but we strive to work with men and women who endeavour to be decent human beings who care more for others than themselves, while still being hard working, driven, and passionate artists and storytellers.

Crystal Lake Publishing is and will always be a beacon of what passion and dedication, combined with overwhelming teamwork and respect, can accomplish. We endeavour to know each and every one of our readers, while building personal relationships with our authors, reviewers, bloggers, podcasters, bookstores, and libraries.

We will be as trustworthy, forthright, and transparent as any business can be, while also keeping most of the headaches away from our authors, since it's our job to solve the problems so they can stay in a creative mind. Which of course also means paying our authors.

We do not just publish books, we present to you worlds within your world, doors within your mind, from talented authors who sacrifice so much for a moment of your time.

There are some amazing small presses out there, and through collaboration and open forums we will continue to support other presses in the goal of helping authors and showing the world what quality small presses are capable of accomplishing. No one wins when a small press goes down, so we will always be there to support hardworking, legitimate presses and their authors. We don't see Crystal Lake as the best press out there, but we will always strive to be the best, strive to be the most interactive and grateful, and even blessed press around. No matter what happens over time, we will also take our mission very seriously while appreciating where we are and enjoying the journey.

What do we offer our authors that they can't do for themselves through self-publishing?

We are big supporters of self-publishing (especially hybrid publishing), if done with care, patience, and planning. However, not every author has the time or inclination to do market research, advertise, and set up book launch strategies. Although a lot of authors are successful in doing it all, strong small presses will always be there for the authors who just want to do what they do best: write.

What we offer is experience, industry knowledge, contacts and trust built up over years. And due to our strong brand and trusting fanbase, every Crystal Lake Publishing book comes with weight of respect. In time our fans begin to trust our judgment and will try a new author purely based on our support of said author.

With each launch we strive to fine-tune our approach, learn from our mistakes, and increase our reach. We continue to assure our authors that we're here for them and that we'll carry the weight of the launch and dealing with third parties while they focus on their strengths—be it writing, interviews, blogs, signings, etc.

We also offer several mentoring packages to authors that include knowledge and skills they can use in both traditional and self-publishing endeavours.

We look forward to launching many new careers.

This is what we believe in. What we stand for. This will be our legacy.

Welcome to Crystal Lake Publishing—
Where stories come alive!

www.ingramcontent.com/pod-product-compliance
Lightning Source LLC
Chambersburg PA
CBHW052112020426
42335CB00021B/2726